Grades 4–8

SCHOLASTIC

Instant PowerPoint® Lessons & Activities

Literary Elements

16 Model Lessons That Guide Students to Create Easy PowerPoint Presentations
That Help Them Analyze Literary Elements in the Books They Read

by Christine Boardman Moen

New York • Toronto • London • Auckland • Sydney
New Delhi • Mexico City • Hong Kong • Buenos Aires

Teaching Resources

Book credits:

From SASSY: LITTLE SISTER IS NOT MY NAME by Sharon M. Draper. Cover art © 2009 by Jackdaw.
Reprinted by permission of Scholastic Inc.

From THE DANGER BOX by Blue Balliett. Cover art © 2010 by Bagram Ibatoulline.
Reprinted by permission of Scholastic Inc.

From MOCKINGJAY by Suzanne Collins. Cover art copyright © 2010 by Tim O'Brien.
Reprinted by permission of Scholastic Inc.

From BONE: OUT OF BONEVILLE by Jeff Smith. Copyright © 2005 by Jeff Smith.
Reprinted by permission of Cartoon Books.

From THE HOUDINI BOX by Brian Selznick. Copyright © 1991 by Brian Selznick.
Published by Atheneum, an imprint of Simon & Schuster.

From THE WATSONS GO TO BIRMINGHAM by Christopher Paul Curtis. Published 1995 by Delacorte Press.

From SWEAR TO HOWDY by Wendelin Van Draanen. Published 2002 by Alfred A. Knopf, Inc.

From THE COMPOSER IS DEAD by Lemony Snicket, illustrated by Carson Ellis.
Illustrations copyright © 2009 by Carson Ellis. Published by HarperCollins Children's Books.

Editor: Maria L. Chang
Designer: Grafica Inc.

ISBN: 978-0-545-33280-4
Copyright © 2012 by Christine Boardman Moen
All rights reserved.
Printed in the U.S.A.

1 2 3 4 5 6 7 8 9 10   40   20 19 18 17 16 15 14 13 12

Contents

Introduction

Welcome to *Instant PowerPoint® Lessons & Activities: Literary Elements*! This book contains all the information you and your students need to create engaging PowerPoint presentations that feature literary elements.

For the last couple of years, I have been strongly encouraging my students to use PowerPoint to demonstrate what they have learned. I did not want their learning to get lost in the use of technology, so I chose PowerPoint over other Web 2.0 technologies because teaching and learning time are valuable; PowerPoint is already loaded onto all our school's computers, and students do not have to spend a lot of time learning how to work the program because it is easy to use and learn. Students create all kinds of PowerPoint presentations—all with an "in-house" program that is easy to use, yet versatile enough to allow for projects that can be simple or simply sensational! As a result of using PowerPoint to teach literary elements, my students not only have learned to recognize and appreciate character, plot, theme, setting, and other literary elements, but are also able to work effectively with others, know how to plan and revise their projects, can comfortably present in front of a group, and can readily evaluate other students' visuals and texts within the PowerPoint format.

How to Use This Book

This book is divided into 16 chapters, each featuring a key literary element. As you work through each chapter, reinforce the learning by encouraging students to look for each literary element in their independent reading and in your read-alouds of novels, short stories, and poems. To help you teach the literary elements using PowerPoint, each chapter in this book includes a convenient teacher page and a reproducible student page that serve as models and guides for the lessons and activities.

Each teacher page offers:
- a detailed explanation of the literary element

- suggestions for introducing the literary element to students

- a specific modeling activity to deepen students' understanding of the literary element

- instructions on how to use the sample PowerPoint on the CD

- an alternative PowerPoint activity to challenge students

Each reproducible student page features:
- a PowerPoint purpose statement

- the suggested number of slides to complete the PowerPoint presentation

- a step-by-step guide to help students produce their own PowerPoint presentation

- a production guide, which is a visual sequence of the PowerPoint presentation with suggestions on what should appear on each slide

Students can complete these projects individually, in pairs, or in small groups. Most of the PowerPoint presentations in this book can be completed using three basic slide layouts and eight different keystrokes (see Command Central, page 72). The PowerPoint slide shows are of various lengths so they can be used with different genres, grade levels, and reading levels.

To help students plan and create their best presentations, provide them with copies of the Planning Pages (pages 12–13), Presentation Checklist (page 14), and Command Central (pages 72–73). It would also be especially helpful to give students copies of the Grading Rubric (pages 10–11) so they know how you will be assessing their projects. Once students have completed their planning pages, allow as long as a week for them to complete their projects. I usually give my students three class periods in the library, where we have a scanner, to create their projects (with appropriate guidance and assistance). Then we schedule their presentations for the following week.

What You Need to Create PowerPoint Presentations

Creating PowerPoint presentations is easy. All you need are the following:

Microsoft® Office PowerPoint®: The student-created PowerPoint activities featured in this book and accompanying CD were made using PowerPoint 2010 for Windows. Use the Command Central list to familiarize yourself with the slide layouts and keystrokes you and your students will use to create the PowerPoint presentations. If you are using PowerPoint 2003 or 2007, the chart on page 7 will help you navigate some of the differences between the versions.

Scanner: Learn to use your school's scanner, whether it is part of a printer or a stand-alone flatbed scanner. Enlist the help of your library-media specialist or technology coordinator to teach students the proper use of the scanning equipment so they can scan images and save them into a file for later use when they create their PowerPoint projects.

LCD Projector: Students will need to project their PowerPoint presentations onto a screen or whiteboard using an LCD (liquid crystal display) projector. These easily connect to computers.

Digital Camera: Students may wish to use a digital camera and add photographs to enhance their PowerPoint presentations. The images on a digital camera can be saved to a computer using a cable or by inserting the camera's SD (Secure Digital) memory card into an enabled printer or configured computer. Once images are saved on the computer, they can easily be imported into a PowerPoint slide show.

Music and Video Files: An easy way to include music in a PowerPoint presentation is to "rip" a song directly from a CD and save it on the computer. Once saved, follow the directions on the Technology Tips sheet (page 74) to insert music into the presentation. To insert a video, you can use one of many programs that can convert digital recordings. However, an easy way to insert video is to use a simple device such as the Flip™ camcorder or any other similar mini camcorder that uploads video to the computer and allows for easy importation of video to a PowerPoint slide show.

> ## CAUTION!
>
> Students may become so intent on adding special effects that their presentations can become cluttered and confusing. It's important to give students the freedom to be creative and add special effects so long as they remain mindful of the purpose. Each presentation should demonstrate and explain a literary element. Inserting elaborate transition "wipes" and colorful word art should not detract from the main message or purpose of the PowerPoint presentation.

Meeting the Common Core State Standards for English Language Arts

The Common Core State Standards for English Language Arts for Grades 4–8 include four broad areas: reading, writing, listening and speaking, and language. The PowerPoint activities and instructional suggestions in this book address numerous areas of the Common Core. Some, but not all, include:

- determining theme
- analyzing alliteration, point of view, irony, and the structure of a poem
- summarizing a text
- citing textual evidence to support the analysis of what the text says
- comparing and contrasting texts in different genres
- using precise language and domain-specific vocabulary
- producing clear and coherent writing appropriate to the task, purpose, and audience
- planning, revising, editing, and rewriting
- drawing evidence from literary or informational texts to support an analysis

The Common Core also addresses the need for student collaboration, so I often have students work in pairs on the projects. If they read the same book, they can work on a project together. If they choose different books but the same literary element, students can create individual PowerPoint slide shows, but use each other as advisors. Students also must speak in front of the class to present their PowerPoint slide shows. Reporting on a topic or text is addressed in the Standards, as well as being able to summarize, use precise language, and include multimedia components and visual displays in presentations. All of this learning is packed into PowerPoint!

For a more complete list of the specific Common Core State Standards the lessons and activities in this book align to, see page 9. Be assured that by providing students the opportunity to create their own PowerPoint presentations to illustrate, demonstrate, and explain essential literary elements, you will be using class time efficiently and effectively. Students will think critically and creatively and be engaged in the introduction, development, and in some cases, the mastery of key Common Core State Standards.

	PowerPoint 2003	PowerPoint 2007
Task Tool Bar	File • Edit • View • Insert • Format • Tools • Slide Show • Window • Help	Home • Insert • Design • Animations • Slide Show • Review • View • Add-Ins
Insert Slide	On the tool bar, select *Insert*, then scroll down and click on *New Slide*. Different slide layout icons will appear on a window on the right. Click on one slide layout to insert into your presentation.	Under the *Home* tab, select *New Slide* from the task bar. Nine different slide layouts will appear. (These are the same as those in the 2010 version.)
Insert Text	While on a blank slide, select *Insert* on the tool bar and scroll down to *Text Box*. Click and drag the cursor to create the text box, then start typing in the box. Use the *Format* tab to change the font or to control line spacing.	While on a blank slide, select the *Insert* tab and a tool bar will appear. Select *Text Box*. Type into the text box. To format the text, select the *Home* tab. You may control spacing by clicking on the *Paragraph* tab. Click on the *Design* tab to add color to slides and type.
Insert Image	Click on *Insert* and scroll down to *Picture*. From there, you can choose *Clip Art*, *From File*, or *From Scanner or Camera*. You can also select *AutoShapes*, *WordArt*, and *Organization Chart*.	Click on the *Insert* tab. You will find the *Picture* icon on the left of the task bar. Click on it, and you will be asked to select an image to insert. Select the image. It will appear on your blank slide and can be moved and resized. (See Command Central on page 72.)

A Word About Copyright and Fair Use

It is important for students to learn about the rules governing copyright and fair use of text, photographs, music, and other digital media. Consider this part of our obligation to teach students about ethics and integrity. Many tools are available to help you and your students understand fair use of copyrighted materials in an educational setting.

Some of the best tools to help you navigate the waters of copyright and fair use are available through the Copyright Advisory Network (http://librarycopyright.net). One helpful tool on its Web site is the Fair Use Evaluator (http://librarycopyright.net/fairuse). By answering a series of questions provided by the Fair Use Evaluator, you and your students can decide if the material you wish to use in a project meets the fair-use criteria. Other useful tools at this same site include the Public Domain Slider and the Exceptions for Instructors eTool.

I have included an easy-to-follow chart (pages 75–76) in the Appendix. Please note that the chart is only a guide. Using copyrighted materials under the fair use clause of the copyright law gives educators and students latitude, but it does not allow for infringement. Consequently, students may use copyrighted materials up to a point for classroom learning purposes, but students' completed PowerPoint presentations may not be posted to the Web if they contain copyrighted images or materials, nor can they be burned onto a CD and distributed.

Final Thoughts

As mentioned, each activity in this book can be completed by students individually, in pairs, or in small groups. This affords you opportunities to differentiate your instruction and use any of the activities to introduce, review, or enrich students' learning. Moreover, students can "show what they know" by first creating a product and then demonstrating their knowledge through a presentation to an audience—both key components in authentic learning. Additionally, the CD that accompanies this book is not only a guide for students but an instructional tool for teachers as well. The sample PowerPoint presentations can be used to teach literary elements and can also serve as visual guides for students to help them create their own presentations. You and your students will find it beneficial to familiarize yourselves with the texts and examples presented on the CD.

Connections With the Common Core State Standards for English Language Arts

The mini-lessons and activities in this book are designed to help you meet your English Language Arts Standards, as well as the Common Core State Standards. For more details on the standards listed below, go to the CCSSI Web site: www.corestandards.org.

Common Core State Standards	Grade 4	Grade 5	Grade 6	Grade 7	Grade 8
Reading Standards for Literature					
Key Ideas and Details	RL.4.1, RL.4.2, RL.4.3	RL.5.1, RL.5.2, RL.5.3	RL.6.1, RL.6.2, RL. 6.3	RL.7.1, RL.7.2, RL.7.3	RL.8.1, RL.8.2, RL.8.3
Craft and Structure	RL.4.4, RL.4.6	RL.5.4, RL.5.5, RL.5.6	RL.6.4, RL.6.6	RL.7.4, RL.7.6	RL.8.4, RL.8.6
Integration of Knowledge and Ideas	RL.4.7	RL.5.7			
Range of Reading and Level of Text Complexity	RL.4.10	RL.5.10	RL.6.10	RL.7.10	RL.8.10
Writing Standards					
Text Types and Purposes	W.4.2, W.4.2b, W.4.2c	W.5.2, W.5.2a, W.5.2b, W.5.2c	W.6.2, W.6.2a, W.6.2b, W.6.2d	W.7.2, W.7.2a, W.7.2b, W.7.2d	W.8.2, W.8.2a, W.8.2b, W.8.2d
Production and Distribution of Writing	W.4.4, W.4.5, W.4.6	W.5.4, W.5.5, W.5.6	W.6.4, W.6.5, W.6.6	W.7.4, W.7.5, W.7.6	W.8.4, W.8.5, W.8.6
Research to Build and Present Knowledge	W.4.9, W.4.9a	W.5.9, W.5.9a	W.6.9, W.6.9a	W.7.9, W.7.9a	W.8.9, W.8.9a
Language Standards					
Conventions of Standard English	L.4.1, L.4.2	L.5.1, L.5.2	L.6.1, L.6.2	L.7.1, L.7.2	L.8.1, L.8.2
Knowledge of Language	L.4.3	L.5.3	L.6.3	L.7.3	L.8.3
Vocabulary Acquisition and Use	L.4.5, L.4.6	L.5.5, L.5.6	L.6.5a, L.6.6	L.7.6	L.8.5a, L.8.6
Speaking and Listening Standards					
Comprehension and Collaboration	SL.4.1, SL.4.2	SL.5.1, SL.5.2	SL.6.1, SL.6.2	SL.7.1, SL.7.2	SL.8.1, SL.8.2
Presentation of Knowledge and Ideas	SL.4.4, SL.4.5, SL.4.6	SL.5.4, SL.5.5, SL.5.6	SL.6.4, SL.6.5	SL.7.4, SL.7.5	SL.8.4, SL.8.5

Grading Rubrics

Use these rubrics to guide students and assess all their PowerPoint presentations.

PowerPoint

Category	Outstanding	Well Done	Meets Requirement	Needs Improvement
Definition of literary element	Definition is well written and exact.	Definition is accurate.	Definition is correct but poorly worded.	Definition is inaccurate.
Support information	Superior examples provide excellent explanation of the literary element.	Very good examples explain the literary element.	Good examples are provided but a more thorough explanation is needed.	Examples are incorrectly used or do not expand on the definition.
Visual appeal; sequencing and number of slides	Each slide is visually appealing. Uses correct sequence and number of slides.	Each slide is well done. Uses nearly correct sequence and number of slides.	Slides are adequate for assignment completion. Sequence and number of slides are adequate.	Slides lack visual appeal as well as necessary information. Sequence and number of slides are inadequate.
Mechanics (spelling, punctuation, grammar)	All mechanics are correct in every aspect.	Mechanics are correct except for minor errors.	There are a few mechanical errors.	There are significant errors in mechanics.

Oral Presentation

Category	Outstanding	Well Done	Meets Requirement	Needs Improvement
Speaking style	Conversational yet polished	Conversational but not well polished	Overall good presentation with few lapses	Read information to the audience
Demeanor and ease with technology	Confident, smooth delivery; practice evident	Practice evident but not polished	Practice evident but relied heavily on notes	Practice not evident; unprepared
Speaking volume	Excellent volume and pronunciation with correct emphasis	Volume suitable for audience and correct enunciation	Volume adequate for presentation; delivery adequate	Inadequate volume; inappropriate delivery
Eye contact	Correct amount of eye contact with audience and the screen	Casual eye contact with audience and the screen	Some contact with audience and the slides and notes	Read from notes and/or the slides

Letter grade or points: _____

Comments: _____

_____

_____

Planning Page

Students, use these pages to plan your PowerPoint presentations.

Instant PowerPoint Lessons & Activities: Literary Elements © 2012 by Christine Boardman Moen, Scholastic Teaching Resources

Planning Page

Instant PowerPoint Lessons & Activities: Literary Elements © 2012 by Christine Boardman Moen, Scholastic Teaching Resources

Presentation Checklist

Keep these tips in mind as you create your PowerPoint presentation.

❑ List or briefly explain key ideas to avoid text overload on your slides.

❑ Left-justify your text instead of centering it, so margins are even and text is easy to read.

❑ Create an eye-appealing slide by balancing the image size and amount of text.

❑ Capitalize only the first word in your sentence or in your lists of ideas.

❑ Use one easy-to-read font style throughout your presentation.

❑ Use bold lettering instead of italics to draw attention to a word or idea.

❑ Use precise vocabulary and use it correctly.

❑ Check each slide for correct spelling, punctuation, and wording.

❑ Use color on your slides only when necessary to avoid confusion or overload.

❑ Transitions do not have to be elaborate. You may wish to simply advance to the next slide.

❑ There is usually an exception to each of the rules above! Check with your teacher!

Keep these tips in mind as you present your PowerPoint presentation.

❑ Practice, practice, practice.

❑ Check the equipment to make sure everything is working before you begin your presentation.

❑ Talk to your audience during your presentation. Do not read your slides to them.

❑ Stand at an angle to your audience so you can gesture to your slides while talking about them. When appropriate, comfortably turn and speak directly to your audience.

❑ If you do not have a hand-held device that you can use to advance your slides, you may wish to have a friend sit at the computer and advance the slides for you. Create a signal or gesture that you will use to indicate when your friend should advance a slide.

❑ Speak clearly and loudly enough for your audience to hear over any equipment that may be running during your presentation.

❑ If you use the Notes feature during your presentation, do not read them to your audience. Any notes, whether on the computer monitor or on index cards in your hand, should be used for reference purposes only.

Instant PowerPoint Lessons & Activities: Literary Elements © 2012 by Christine Boardman Moen, Scholastic Teaching Resources

Character

Character Qualities

Students provide text support for three character traits that reveal the story's main character.

The Element Explained

A story's main *character* can be a person, animal, or even an object. Authors reveal a character through his or her thoughts, actions, and words as well as the character's physical appearance and what others say or think about him or her. A story's characters have qualities just like humans do. Some characters are brave, honest, and courageous, while others may be fearful, mistrustful, and dishonest. Recognizing the main character's qualities is a helpful aid to reading comprehension.

Introducing the Literary Element

- Students are familiar with famous American leaders Abraham Lincoln and Martin Luther King, Jr. Working in groups of three, have students write the names of these two leaders on opposite sides of a sheet of paper and list qualities they believe each leader possessed. Then invite each group to read their list aloud. Create a master list on chart paper. As students name each quality, prompt them to support that attribute with examples from Lincoln's or King's life.

- Invite students to work in pairs to play a game called "What Kind of Qualities Does It Take?" Call out a specific situation or circumstance and challenge students to list at least two character qualities needed to handle that situation. For example, *What kind of qualities does it take to rescue someone who is trapped in snow or a mine? To give blood to a blood bank?*

Modeling Activity

On strips of paper, write the names of various character qualities, both desirable and undesirable, such as kind, loyal, friendly, dishonest, greedy, and lazy. Make sure you have at least one strip for each student. Put the strips in a jar and invite each student to draw one. Then ask students to draw a representation of what they think the character quality looks like. For example, "friendly" could be represented by a big smile, whereas "unfriendly" could be a cold stare or pursed lips. Display the drawings along with the labels of the character qualities.

Introducing the PowerPoint Activity

Tell students they will create a short PowerPoint presentation to show what they know about character qualities, using stories they've chosen (or you've assigned). Hand out copies of "What a Character!" (page 16) and review the steps and production guide. Show students the model PowerPoint presentation "Character" from the CD.

Alternative Presentation

Have students select a character trait and name fictional characters as well as historical people who possess this character quality. Students must always provide examples to support their analysis. For example, for "courage" students could include George Washington, Ruby Bridges, Sally Ride, Anne Frank, and Katniss Everdeen from The Hunger Games series.

What a Character!

PowerPoint Purpose

Identify three character traits or qualities that the main character of your book possesses and support each quality with examples from the text.

Number of Slides

8 to 10 slides (If you need more or fewer slides, discuss options with your teacher.)

Creating the PowerPoint Presentation

1. Scan your book's cover or your own related artwork and insert the image into the opening *Title and Content* slide. Type the title "Character Qualities" in the boxed area at the top of the slide.

2. Select the *Content with Caption* layout for the next slide. Insert the book cover image or artwork on the right side of the slide. On the left side, type the book's title in the smaller top box. Type the author's name, publisher, and copyright date in the larger box below it. Center the text and space the words out to make the whole slide look attractive.

3. Select a blank slide and insert a text box. Write a concise definition of the literary element "character," including an explanation of character qualities.

4. Add another blank slide and insert a text box. Identify a character quality of your main character. Make sure you include support from the text. Use quotation marks and page number(s).

5. Repeat Step 4 two more times to supply a second and a third example of a character quality with text support. If you wish to insert any art or illustrations, use the *Insert Picture* command.

6. Create a "wrap-up" slide that restates the three character qualities.

7. Repeat your opening slide to finish up your presentation.

Instant PowerPoint Lessons & Activities: Literary Elements © 2012 by Christine Boardman Moen, Scholastic Teaching Resources

Follow this basic format to meet the requirements for this assignment.

SLIDE 1: Book cover or artwork

SLIDE 2: Cover, title, author, publisher, copyright date

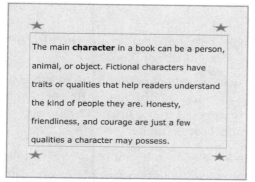

SLIDE 3: Definition of character and character qualities

SLIDE 4: First character quality with text support

SLIDE 5: Second character quality with text support

SLIDE 6: Third character quality with text support

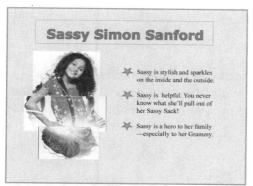

SLIDE 7: All three character qualities listed

SLIDE 8: Final slide

Setting

Clues to Help Clarify

Students explain the setting of their story, noting clues from the text as support.

The Element Explained

The time period in which a story takes place and the location of the story's events make up the *setting*. Often, a story would not be the same if the events occurred within the context of a different setting. This is especially true of historical fiction, which weaves real historical events, places, and people into a fictional story line.

Introducing the Literary Element

- Read aloud the beginning of a variety of stories and books with different settings and invite students to identify the clues that pinpoint the setting of each story and book.

- Copy the chart below on the board. Invite students to use their imagination to fill in the chart with their own settings and characters. Next, have students exchange charts and write opening lines to a story that include clues to the setting. For example, a story set in the future (2090), at a place called Planet 16A, and with characters named Zem-1 and Troy could be:

  The celebration day, although perfectly sunny and spring-like, was beginning on a sour note. Troy scrambled to dab polish on his scuffed boots, grumbling that his personal robot assistant, Zem-1, had yet again malfunctioned. Troy hurried. He didn't want to be late for the opening ceremony that officially marked the renaming of Earth's newest satellite community, Planet 16A. The community's new name? Serenity, of course!

Time	Place	Name(s) of Character(s)
Past		
Present		
Future		

Modeling Activity

Have students create personal business cards that indicate where they'll be living and what their occupation or profession will be ten years after they graduate from high school. Then put students into groups and have them exchange cards and discuss the "setting" of their future personal stories.

Introducing the PowerPoint Activity

Tell students they will create a short PowerPoint presentation to show what they know about setting, using the stories they've chosen (or you've assigned). Hand out copies of "A Time and a Place for Everything" (page 19) and review the steps and production guide. Show students the model PowerPoint presentation "Setting" from the CD.

Alternative Presentation

Have students create a PowerPoint presentation that identifies settings of different books that feature the past, the present, and the future.

A Time and a Place for Everything

PowerPoint Purpose

Describe the setting of your book by identifying the time period and location in which the story takes place. Provide support from the text for your conclusions.

Number of Slides

10 to 12 slides (If you need more or fewer slides, discuss options with your teacher.)

Creating the PowerPoint Presentation

1. Scan your book's cover or your own related artwork and insert the image into the opening *Title and Content* slide. Type the title "Setting" in the boxed area at the top of the slide.

2. Select the *Content with Caption* layout. Insert the book cover image or artwork on the right side of the slide. On the left side, type the book's title in the smaller top box. Type the author's name, publisher, and copyright date in the larger box below it. Center the text and space the words out to make the whole slide look attractive.

3. Select a blank slide and insert a text box. Write a brief definition of the literary element "setting."

4. Select another blank slide, insert a text box, and explain the elements of "time" and "place" as part of the setting.

5. On the next blank slide, list several clues from the text that support your conclusion about the time period during which the story takes place. (In the sample slide, arrows created using the Shape tool highlight each supporting idea.) Use another slide to provide additional support from your text to explain the time setting of your story.

6. On the next two or three slides, use text support to indicate the time and location of the story. For clarity, insert an image.

7. Add another blank slide and insert two text boxes—one for time and the other for place. In them summarize your supporting information and draw a conclusion about the story's setting.

8. Repeat your opening slide to finish up your presentation.

Production Guide

Follow this basic format to meet the requirements for this assignment.

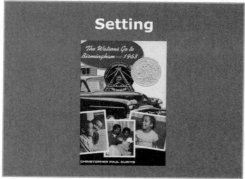

SLIDE 1: Book cover or artwork

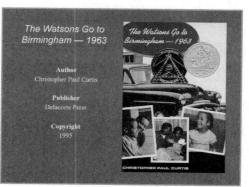

SLIDE 2: Cover, title, author, publisher, copyright date

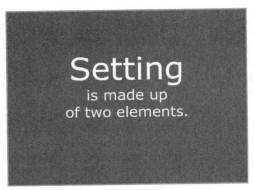

SLIDE 3: Definition of setting

SLIDE 4: Explanation of setting as time and place

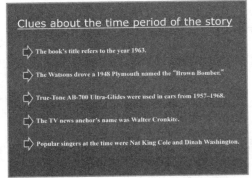

SLIDE 5: List of text clues that identify the time period of the setting

SLIDE 6: Text clue that describes the setting

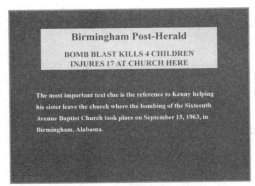

SLIDE 7: Another text clue that describes the setting

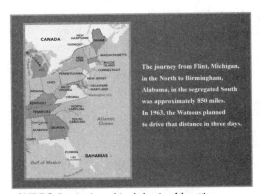

SLIDE 8: Text clue that explains the location of the setting

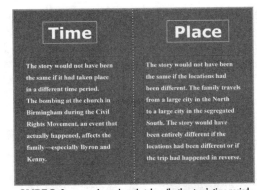

SLIDE 9: Summary of text clues that describe the story's time period and location

SLIDE 10: Final slide

Instant PowerPoint Lessons & Activities: Literary Elements © 2012 by Christine Boardman Moen, Scholastic Teaching Resources

Plot

One Scene Leads to Another

Students retell a story's plot from the beginning through the middle and to the end.

The Element Explained

The *plot* of a story includes the events that make up the story itself. One event typically leads to another, unless the plot is interrupted with a flashback. All stories have a beginning, middle, and end. A more formal analysis of plot includes:

Introduction—The beginning of the story usually describes the characters, conflict, and setting.

Rising Action—A series of events builds up to a climax. The rising action is longer and more complicated than the falling action.

Climax—At this point of the story, an outcome must occur. As a result of what happens in the climax, the conflict will be resolved, whether in a positive or a negative way.

Falling Action—Following the climax, events progress rapidly and loose ends are tied up. The falling action should lead logically to the resolution.

Resolution—The conflict is resolved and the story ends. Sometimes in stories, not resolving the conflict is the resolution itself.

Introducing the Literary Element

- Provide students with sticky notes and several picture books and/or age-appropriate short stories. Have students divide the stories into "beginning," "middle," and "end" and label them accordingly. Then invite students to share their stories and explain how they decided on where the labels belong.

- Have students work in pairs or small groups to create original stories. Using colored note cards, have them list introductory information, rising action events, the climax, falling action events, and the resolution. When finished, have students shuffle their cards and exchange them with another group's. Then challenge students to put the cards in order and retell the group's story.

Modeling Activity

Distribute a set of note cards that list the formal elements of plot based on your chosen read-aloud story. As you read, students come forward and place their cards under one of the five plot element headings, which you have created on the board. When finished, review the cards. Ask students to explain their decisions for the placement of their cards. Make adjustments if necessary for clarity.

Introducing the PowerPoint Activity

Tell students they will create a short PowerPoint presentation to show what they know about plot, using the stories they've chosen (or you've assigned). Hand out copies of "The Plot Thickens!" (page 22) and review the steps and production guide. Show students the model PowerPoint presentation "Plot" from the CD.

Alternative Presentation

Have students write and illustrate original stories and identify the plot elements.

The Plot Thickens!

PowerPoint Purpose

Define the literary element of plot and analyze the plot of a story, breaking the story's events into informal categories (beginning, middle, end) or formal categories (introduction, rising action, climax, falling action, resolution).

Number of Slides

8 to 15 slides (If you need more or fewer slides, discuss options with your teacher.)

Creating the PowerPoint Presentation

1. Scan your book's cover or your own related artwork and insert the image into the opening *Title and Content* slide. Type the title "Plot" in the boxed area at the top of the slide.

2. Select the *Content with Caption* layout for the next slide. Insert the book cover image or artwork on the right side of the slide. On the left side, type the book's title in the smaller top box. Type the author's name, publisher, and copyright date in the larger box below it. Center the text and space the words out to make the whole slide look attractive.

3. Select a blank slide and insert a text box. Write a concise definition of the literary element "plot."

4. If you are doing a formal analysis of plot, add another blank slide and identify the five elements that make up a formal plot line. If you are doing an informal analysis, you may skip this step.

5. Select another blank slide, insert a text box, and summarize your book's introductory information, including the characters, setting, and conflict.

6. On the next two (for informal) to four (for formal) slides, describe the middle events of the story or rising action.

7. After you have described the middle events or rising action, use another blank slide to describe the climactic event of the story.

8. On the next blank slide, write the ending of the story if you're doing an informal analysis. If doing the formal analysis, use one to three slides to describe the events that make up the falling action of the story, then another slide to describe how the conflict was resolved. This is your resolution slide.

9. Repeat your opening slide to finish up your presentation.

Production Guide

Follow this basic format to meet the requirements for this assignment.

INFORMAL

SLIDE 1: Book cover or artwork

Instant PowerPoint Lessons & Activities: Literary Elements © 2012 by Christine Boardman Moen, Scholastic Teaching Resources

SLIDE 2: Cover, title, author, publisher, copyright date

The **plot** includes the events in the story.

These events combine to make up a story.

Every story has a beginning, middle, and end.

SLIDE 3: Definition of plot

BEGINNING

In the early 1900's, ten-year old Victor dreams of becoming a magician like the famous Houdini.

SLIDE 4: Beginning information: character(s), conflict, and setting

MIDDLE

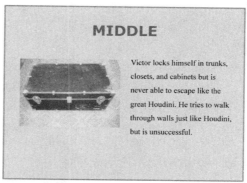

Victor locks himself in trunks, closets, and cabinets but is never able to escape like the great Houdini. He tries to walk through walls just like Houdini, but is unsuccessful.

SLIDE 5: Description of middle event

MIDDLE

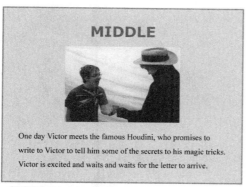

One day Victor meets the famous Houdini, who promises to write to Victor to tell him some of the secrets to his magic tricks. Victor is excited and waits and waits for the letter to arrive.

SLIDE 6: Description of middle event

CLIMAX

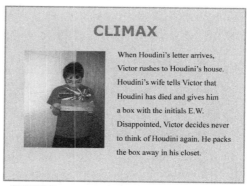

When Houdini's letter arrives, Victor rushes to Houdini's house. Houdini's wife tells Victor that Houdini has died and gives him a box with the initials E.W. Disappointed, Victor decides never to think of Houdini again. He packs the box away in his closet.

SLIDE 7: Description of climactic event

END

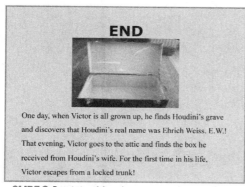

One day, when Victor is all grown up, he finds Houdini's grave and discovers that Houdini's real name was Ehrich Weiss. E.W.! That evening, Victor goes to the attic and finds the box he received from Houdini's wife. For the first time in his life, Victor escapes from a locked trunk!

SLIDE 8: Description of the end

Plot

SLIDE 9: Final slide

FORMAL

SLIDE 1: Book cover or artwork

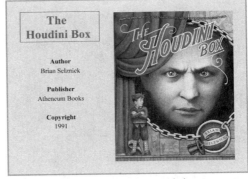

SLIDE 2: Cover, title, author, publisher, copyright date

The **plot** includes the events in the story.

These events combine to make up a story.

Every story has a beginning, middle, and end.

SLIDE 3: Definition of plot

A more formal way of describing **plot**

is to divide a story into parts:

INTRODUCTION

RISING ACTION

CLIMAX

FALLING ACTION

RESOLUTION

SLIDE 4: Formal listing of five elements of plot

INTRODUCTION

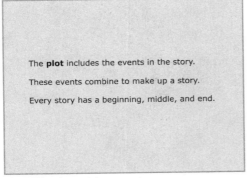

In the early 1900's, ten-year old Victor dreams of becoming a magician like the famous Houdini.

SLIDE 5: Introduction including character(s), conflict, and setting

---

RISING ACTION

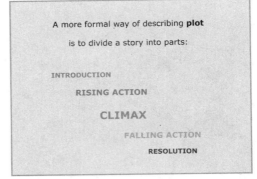

Victor locks himself in trunks, closets, and cabinets but is never able to escape like the great Houdini.

SLIDE 6: Description of rising action event

RISING ACTION

Victor learns that Houdini can hold his breath under water for 5,000 seconds! Victor tries to practice holding his breath while in the bathtub, but his mom makes him get out and breathe.

SLIDE 7: Description of rising action event

RISING ACTION

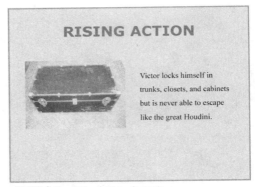

Victor tries to walk through walls just like Houdini. Victor is unsuccessful.

SLIDE 8: Description of rising action event

RISING ACTION

One day Victor meets the famous Houdini, who promises to write to Victor to tell him some of the secrets to his magic tricks. Victor is excited and waits and waits for the letter to arrive.

SLIDE 9: Description of rising action event

CLIMAX

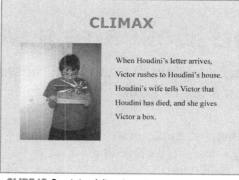

When Houdini's letter arrives, Victor rushes to Houdini's house. Houdini's wife tells Victor that Houdini has died, and she gives Victor a box.

SLIDE 10: Description of climactic event

FALLING ACTION

The initials E.W. are on the box. Victor is so disappointed that he makes up his mind never to think of Houdini again. He packs the box away in his closet.

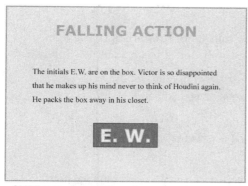

SLIDE 11: Description of falling action event

FALLING ACTION

Victor grows up, gets married, and has a son. One evening when Victor and his son are playing ball, Victor's son hits his baseball into a nearby graveyard.

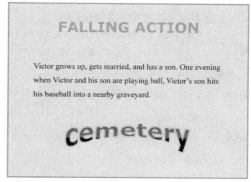

SLIDE 12: Description of falling action event

FALLING ACTION

When Victor and his son go to get the ball, Victor finds the ball resting on Houdini's grave. This is when Victor learns Houdini's real name was Ehrich Weiss. Houdini's real initials were E.W.!

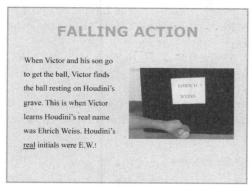

SLIDE 13: Description of falling action event

RESOLUTION

That evening, Victor goes to the attic and finds the box he received from Houdini's wife. For the first time in his life, Victor escapes from a locked trunk!

SLIDE 14: Description of resolution

Plot

SLIDE 15: Final slide

Theme

The Message's Meaning

Students explain the universal message woven into the fabric of their story or book.

The Element Explained

A story's *theme* is its overall message to the reader. A story's theme is based on a topic, such as family, friendship, or identity. However, a story's theme is broader than a topic and can be stated in a sentence or two.

Introducing the Literary Element

- Share different Aesop fables, but explain the themes or morals of the fables using age-appropriate messages. Stories with themes that appeal to students in Grades 4–8 include:

  "The Fox and the Stork"
  Theme: Playing a joke on someone may be funny until the joke is played on you.

  "The Lion and the Mouse"
  Theme: Don't hesitate to be kind because that kindness may be returned to you someday.

  "The Boy Who Cried Wolf"
  Theme: Once people recognize you as a liar, they won't trust you even when you're telling the truth.

- Read aloud Helen Ketterman's *Armadilly Chili* (Albert Whitman, 2004) with its theme of "Life is better with friends to share it with." For older students, read *Sélavi, That Is Life: A Haitian Story of Hope* by Youme Landowne (Cinco Puntos Press, 2004) with its theme, "Remaining hopeful is necessary even under extremely difficult living conditions."

Modeling Activity

Divide the class into small groups. Present student groups with one of the following themes and invite them to create a story that conveys the message. Have students act out their story, read it aloud, or present the story in a Readers' Theater format.

- Friends are like elevators. They can take you up or they can take you down.
- People who regularly cheat in small matters may end up cheating in bigger matters.

Introducing the PowerPoint Activity

Tell students they will create a short PowerPoint presentation to show what they know about theme, using the stories they've chosen (or you've assigned). Hand out copies of "There's a Theme Here" (page 27) and review the steps and production guide. Show students the model PowerPoint presentation "Theme" from the CD.

Alternative Presentation

If they wish, allow students to write their own theme statement and create a story-driven PowerPoint presentation.

There's a Theme Here

PowerPoint Purpose
Explain a story's theme or basic message, expressing the theme in a complete sentence or two. Support your theme statement with examples from the story and explanations or observations of your own.

Number of Slides
10 to 15 slides (If you need more or fewer slides, discuss options with your teacher.)

Creating the PowerPoint Presentation

1. Scan your book's cover or your own related artwork and insert the image into your opening *Title and Content* slide. Type the title "Theme" in the boxed area at the top of the slide.

2. Select the *Content with Caption* layout for the next slide. Insert the book cover image or artwork on the right side of the slide. On the left side, type the book's title in the smaller top box. Type the author's name, publisher, and copyright date in the larger box below it. Center these and space the words out to make the whole slide look attractive.

3. Select a blank slide and insert a text box. Write a concise definition of the literary element "theme."

4. Add another blank slide, insert a text box, and write a sample theme statement from another text you have read. It can be a book or a poem. Use the *Insert Picture* command to insert the sample book's cover image or your own artwork.

5. On the next blank slide, write a concise theme statement for the book you are featuring in this PowerPoint presentation.

6. On the next three slides, provide examples from the story that support your theme statement. Use quotation marks and page numbers when necessary.

7. Restate your book's theme statement.

8. Repeat your opening slide to finish up your presentation.

Instant PowerPoint Lessons & Activities: Literary Elements © 2012 by Christine Boardman Moen, Scholastic Teaching Resources

Follow this basic format to meet the requirements for this assignment.

SLIDE 1: Book cover or artwork

SLIDE 2: Cover, title, author, publisher, copyright date

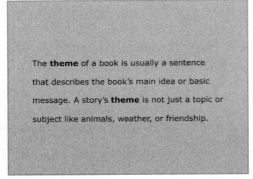

SLIDE 3: Definition of theme

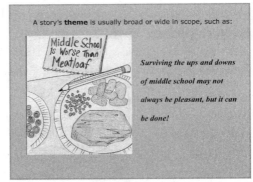

SLIDE 4: Example theme statement based on another text

SLIDE 5: Theme statement of text you've chosen for presentation

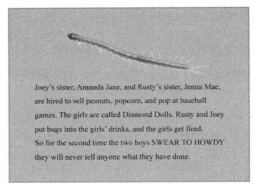

SLIDE 6: Example from the text to support your theme statement

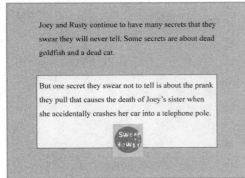

SLIDE 7: Example from the text to support your theme statement

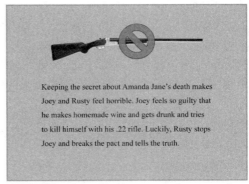

SLIDE 8: Example from the text to support your theme statement

Joey does not forgive Rusty for breaking the pact, and they aren't friends anymore. Joey wonders if he did the right thing.

"And it made me wonder what being a true friend actually meant. Had I messed up for good, breakin' the pact? But how could a true friend let things go on?"

(page 121)

SLIDE 9: Example from the text to support your theme statement

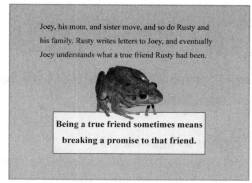

Joey, his mom, and sister move, and so do Rusty and his family. Rusty writes letters to Joey, and eventually Joey understands what a true friend Rusty had been.

Being a true friend sometimes means breaking a promise to that friend.

SLIDE 10: Restatement of book's theme

SLIDE 11: Final slide

Conflict

In the Driver's Seat

Students identify and illustrate four basic types of conflict that drive stories to their conclusion.

The Element Explained

Every story must have *conflict* in order to move the story to its resolution. Conflict is the struggle between two or more opposing forces. Stories often have more than one conflict, but there's usually one main or overriding conflict. The four basic types of conflict are:

Person Against Person: Two characters (usually one is the main character) are in conflict.

Person Against Nature: The character is fighting a force of nature, such as flood or famine.

Person Against Self: The character has conflicting feelings or thoughts.

Person Against Society: The character is in conflict with laws or beliefs of the majority.

Introducing the Literary Element

Read aloud picture books or age-appropriate short stories that illustrate each of the four types of conflict. Some choices may include:

Person Against Person: *Art & Max* by David Wiesner (Clarion, 2010)

Person Against Nature: *The Buffalo Are Back* by Jean Craighead George (Dutton, 2010)

Person Against Self: *Elsie's Bird* by Jane Yolen and David Small (Philomel, 2010)

Person Against Society: *Dave the Potter: Artist, Poet, Slave* by Laban Carrick Hill (Little, Brown, 2010)

Modeling Activity

Put together a collection of 16 young adult or middle readers that are good examples of conflict. Be sure to include four books for each type of conflict: Person Against Person, Person Against Nature, Person Against Self, and Person Against Society. Play "Sort and Stand" with the class. Designate the four corners of the classroom with a specific type of conflict. Give each student a book and ask him or her to read the jacket cover, decide its main conflict, and stand in the appropriate corner with the book. Students must explain their choice of conflict based on the jacket information. Students who have read the selected books may support or correct students' guesses.

Introducing the PowerPoint Activity

Tell students they will create a short PowerPoint presentation to show what they know about conflict from the books they've chosen (or you've assigned). Hand out copies of "Conflict of Interest" (page 31) and review the steps and production guide. Show students the model PowerPoint presentation "Conflict" from the CD.

Alternative Presentation

Challenge students to demonstrate how a change in conflict alters other literary elements, such as character, plot, and mood.

Conflict of Interest

PowerPoint Purpose

Identify examples of each of the four types of conflict and support each example with textual references.

Number of Slides

14 to 20 slides (If you need more or fewer slides, discuss options with your teacher.)

Creating the PowerPoint Presentation

1. Scan your book's cover or your own related artwork and insert the image into your opening *Title and Content* slide. Type the title "Conflict" in the boxed area at the top of the slide.

2. Select the *Content with Caption* layout for the next slide. Insert the book cover image or artwork on the right side of the slide. On the left side, type the book's title in the smaller top box. Type the author's name, publisher, and copyright date in the larger box below it. Center the text and space the words out to make the whole slide look attractive.

3. Select a blank slide and insert a text box. Write a concise definition of the literary element "conflict."

4. If you choose to use one book to demonstrate all four types of conflict, select a blank slide and insert the cover of your book and a text box. In the text box, summarize your book so your audience will be able to understand your examples in context.

5. Select the *Title Only* layout for the next slide and type "Person Against Person" in the top bar. Insert a text box below and provide an example from the book. Remember to use quotation marks and identify the page from the text.

6. If you wish, use another *Title Only* slide to expand on the example in the previous slide, provide a second example from the text, or display related artwork.

7. Repeat Steps 5 and 6 three more times to supply examples of Person Against Nature, Person Against Self, and Person Against Society.

8. Add a slide with the *Title Only* layout. In the top bar, type "Conflicts in the book [insert book title]." Insert a text box below and briefly summarize the examples from the book that illustrate the four different types of conflict.

9. Repeat your opening slide to finish up your presentation.

Follow this basic format to meet the requirements for this assignment.

SLIDE 1: Book cover or artwork

SLIDE 2: Cover, title, author, publisher, copyright date

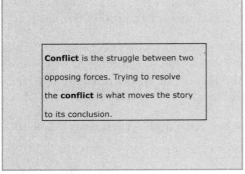

> **Conflict** is the struggle between two opposing forces. Trying to resolve the **conflict** is what moves the story to its conclusion.

SLIDE 3: Definition of conflict

Four types of **conflict** are represented in this story.

In present-day Massachusetts, Franklin Smith, a popular athlete from a prominent family, is accidentally killed. A Cambodian immigrant, Chay Chouan, confesses. The paths of Chay and Franklin's younger brother, Henry, cross as Henry decides to climb Mount Katahdin, a trip he had planned with his brother.

SLIDE 4: Overview of text with artwork or cover

Person Against Person

Franklin Smith attacks Chay Chouan because Franklin does not believe Chay, a Cambodian immigrant, should be seeing his sister, who is from a founding family of the small Massachusetts town of Blythbury-by-the-Sea.

SLIDE 5: Example of Person Against Person

Person Against Person

In an act of revenge for the accidental killing of his brother, Henry pummels Chay, who offers no resistance.

SLIDE 6: Second example of Person Against Person

Person Against Society

Chay, a Cambodian immigrant, and Louisa, a girl whose family is among the founding families of Blythbury-by-the-Sea, attend the same college prep school. The two fall in love, but their love is in conflict with the beliefs of many who feel that Chay has no right to have feelings for a girl of Louisa's social status. At the same time, their love is unacceptable to Chay's Cambodian family.

SLIDE 7: Example of Person Against Society

Person Against Society

In a conversation about loving a person from a different culture or ethnic background, Chay tells Henry:

"If I brought home an American girl, my family would not get used to it. They'd say American girls are immoral. They'd say an American girl would disgrace the family. They'd say they could never go back to Cambodia with honor and respect."

(page 217)

SLIDE 8: Second example of Person Against Society

Person Against Nature

Despite being injured, Henry, his sister Louisa, and his friend Sandborn climb Mount Katahdin.

"... all three finally took the last short, knee-knocking steps onto the peak and looked out. The top ridges of Katahdin undulated around them ..."

(page 291)

SLIDE 9: Example of Person Against Nature

Person Against Nature

Henry rescues Black Dog from the crashing waves in the cove near his home. They both nearly drown when Black Dog overturns Henry's kayak.

SLIDE 10: Second example of Person Against Nature

Person Against Self

Henry wants to hate Chay for the accidental death of his brother Franklin. But Henry learns that Chay is guilt-ridden not only about the accident but also about the loss of his family's love.

SLIDE 11: Example of Person Against Self

Person Against Self

Before his death, Franklin told Henry that Henry was too weak and not "man enough" to climb Katahdin with him. When Franklin died, Henry was determined to make the climb to prove to himself that he could do it.

"How could he explain to his parents that there was something about climbing Katahdin that was important? That it was so important, that fire burned in his guts?"

(page 146)

SLIDE 12: Second example of Person Against Self

Conflicts in the book *Trouble*

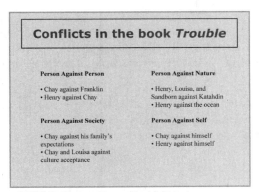

Person Against Person

• Chay against Franklin
• Henry against Chay

Person Against Society

• Chay against his family's expectations
• Chay and Louisa against culture acceptance

Person Against Nature

• Henry, Louisa, and Sandborn against Katahdin
• Henry against the ocean

Person Against Self

• Chay against himself
• Henry against himself

SLIDE 13: Summary of four conflicts found in book

Conflict

SLIDE 14: Final slide

First Person, Second Person & Third-Person Limited

Students identify and explain the use of different points of view.

The Element Explained

Three basic *points of view* authors use are first person, second person, and third-person limited.

First Person: The narrator is the main character, using pronouns such as *I, me, our, we,* and *my.*

Second Person: The author speaks directly to the reader, using the pronoun *you.* Second person is often used in articles that give advice or instructions.

Third-Person Limited: The author uses a narrator who is not a character in the story but who is able to tell what the main character is thinking and feeling. The author uses pronouns such as *he, she,* and *they.*

Introducing the Literary Element

Read aloud portions of short stories, novels, or picture books and have students identify from whose point of view the story is being told. Students should note the author's use of pronouns.

First Person: *Yatandou* by Gloria Whelan (Sleeping Bear Press, 2007)

Second Person: *How to Survive in Antarctica* by Lucy Jane Bledsoe (Holiday House, 2006)

Third-Person Limited: *14 Cows for America* by Carmen Agra Deedy (Peachtree, 2009)

Modeling Activity

Have students select a book, copy the opening few lines, and identify the book's point of view. Then have them rewrite the opening lines using a different point of view. This example is from *Henry's Freedom Box* by Ellen Levine (Scholastic, 2007).

Original Third Person:

Henry Brown wasn't sure how old he was. Henry was a slave. And slaves weren't allowed to know their birthdays.

Rewrite First Person:

My name is Henry Brown. I don't know how old I am. I am a slave, and slaves aren't allowed to know their birthdays.

Introducing the PowerPoint Activity

Tell students they will create a short PowerPoint presentation to show what they know about point of view, using the stories they've chosen (or you've assigned). Hand out copies of "What's Your Point of View?" (page 35) and review the steps and production guide. Show students the model PowerPoint presentation "Point of View" from CD.

Alternative Presentation

Have students select a short poem written in the first person and rewrite it in second and third persons. On their presentation, have them explain how the changes impacted the poem's meaning and rhythm.

What's Your Point of View?

PowerPoint Purpose

Provide examples of different texts that use the first-person, second-person, and third-person limited points of view, or select a text that features all three points of view. Provide textual support for each example.

Number of Slides

8 to 10 slides (If you need more or fewer slides, discuss options with your teacher.)

Creating the PowerPoint Presentation

1. Scan and insert an image into the opening *Title and Content* slide that represents point of view. Type the title "Point of View" in the boxed area at the top of the slide. Identify the three points of view and define "point of view."

2. Select the *Content with Caption* layout for the next slide. Scan and insert the first book cover image or your own related artwork on the right side of the slide. On the left side, type the book's title in the smaller top box. Type the author's name, publisher, and copyright date in the larger box below it. Center the text and space the words out to make the whole slide look attractive.

3. Select a blank slide and insert a text box. Provide an example from the text that shows the first person point of view. Remember to use quotation marks and page numbers.

4. Repeat Steps 2 and 3 with another book that uses the second-person point of view.

5. Choose a book that uses the third-person limited point of view, and repeat Steps 2 and 3.

6. Repeat your opening slide to finish up your presentation.

*Note: The accompanying production guide features a book in which all three points of view are used.

Instant PowerPoint Lessons & Activities: Literary Elements © 2012 by Christine Boardman Moen, Scholastic Teaching Resources

Follow this basic format to meet the requirements for this assignment.

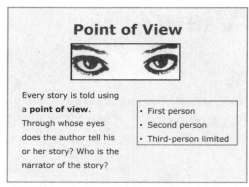

SLIDE 1: Artwork or image, point of view definition, including list of three points of view

SLIDE 2: Cover, title, author, publisher, copyright date

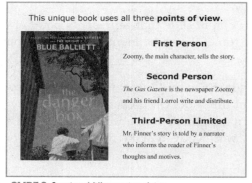

SLIDE 3: Overview of different points of view

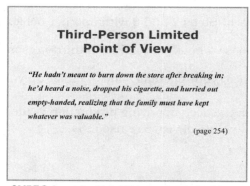

SLIDE 4: Example from book of first point of view

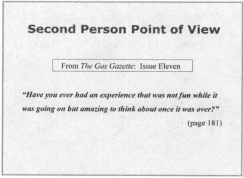

SLIDE 5: Example from book of second-person point of view

SLIDE 6: Example from book of third-person limited point of view

SLIDE 7: More examples from other books

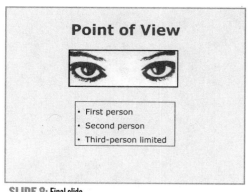

SLIDE 8: Final slide

Mood

Developing an Atmosphere

Students use text clues to explain the mood of a text.

The Element Explained

An author develops *mood*—the emotional atmosphere of a book—by carefully selecting words and details to include in his or her work. For example, an author may develop a humorous mood by using puns or other words that convey humor, as well as details that are likely to make the reader laugh out loud. Funny, sad, frightened, delighted—these are just a few of the many moods authors create through word choice and details.

Introducing the Literary Element

• Read aloud a humorous poem and ask students to identify words and phrases that make the poem funny. Then provide contrast by reading a poem with an entirely different mood and have students identify how the poet created that atmosphere.

• Play musical excerpts that convey different moods. Invite students to supply words to describe the music.

Modeling Activity

Play a game called "Judge a Book by Its Cover." Select specific books with exceptional covers. Show the class each cover and ask students to write words describing the mood they think the cover conveys. Also ask students to describe some possible details the book's story may include. Ask students who have read the book to confirm classmates' word choices and details, or read the inside jacket or a book review to confirm or challenge students' ideas.

Introducing the PowerPoint Activity

Tell students they will create a short PowerPoint presentation to show what they know about mood, using the book they've chosen (or you've assigned). Hand out copies of "In the Mood" (page 38) and review the steps and production guide. Show students the model PowerPoint presentation "Mood" from the CD.

Alternative Presentation

Have students select different texts written by the same author, but with each text having a different mood. Ask students to contrast the two (or more) texts using selected word choices and specific examples from the texts to support their analysis of each text's mood. Suggest versatile authors, such as Jane Yolen, who writes poetry, historical fiction, and fantasy.

In the Mood

PowerPoint Purpose
Provide examples from the text illustrating the author's use of words and details to create a specific mood.

Number of Slides
8 to 10 slides (If you need more or fewer slides, discuss options with your teacher.)

Creating the PowerPoint Presentation

1. Scan your book's cover or your own related artwork and insert the image into your opening *Title and Content* slide. Type the title "Mood" in the boxed area at the top of the slide.

2. Select the *Content with Caption* layout for the next slide. Insert the book cover image or artwork on the right side of the screen. On the left side, type the book's title in the smaller top box. Type the author's name, publisher, and copyright date in the large box below it. Center the text and space the words out to make the whole slide look attractive.

3. Select a blank slide and insert a text box. Write a concise definition of the literary element "mood."

4. Add another blank slide and insert a text box. Explain the mood of the book you are using to illustrate this literary element.

5. On the next blank slide, provide an example from the text that illustrates that mood. Make sure to use quotation marks and identify the page number(s).

6. Repeat Step 5 two more times to provide a second and a third example from the text that illustrate the mood of your book. If you wish to insert any art or illustrations, use the *Insert Picture* command.

7. Repeat your opening slide to finish up your presentation.

Instant PowerPoint Lessons & Activities: Literary Elements © 2012 by Christine Boardman Moen, Scholastic Teaching Resources

Follow this basic format to meet the requirements for this assignment.

SLIDE 1: Book cover

SLIDE 2: Cover, title, author's name, publisher, copyright date

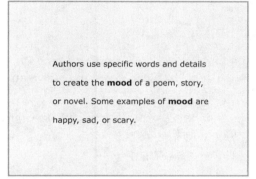

Authors use specific words and details to create the **mood** of a poem, story, or novel. Some examples of **mood** are happy, sad, or scary.

SLIDE 3: Definition of mood as a literary element

The mood of *Deep and Dark and Dangerous* is reflected in its title as well as the book's cover. The mood is eerie and goes well with a ghost story. Words and details that the author uses to build this mood include the following.

SLIDE 4: Description of the mood of the book

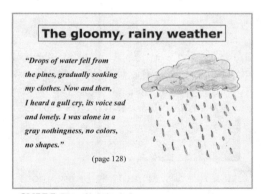

The gloomy, rainy weather

"Drops of water fell from the pines, gradually soaking my clothes. Now and then, I heard a gull cry, its voice sad and lonely. I was alone in a gray nothingness, no colors, no shapes."

(page 128)

SLIDE 5: First example from text

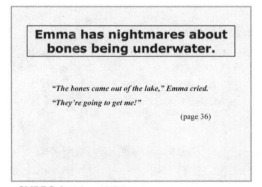

Emma has nightmares about bones being underwater.

"The bones came out of the lake," Emma cried. "They're going to get me!"

(page 36)

SLIDE 6: Second example from text

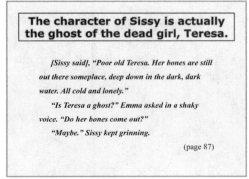

The character of Sissy is actually the ghost of the dead girl, Teresa.

[Sissy said], "Poor old Teresa. Her bones are still out there someplace, deep down in the dark, dark water. All cold and lonely."

"Is Teresa a ghost?" Emma asked in a shaky voice. "Do her bones come out?"

"Maybe." Sissy kept grinning.

(page 87)

SLIDE 7: Third example from text

SLIDE 8: Final slide

Foreshadowing

Hinting at Future Events

Students provide examples of foreshadowing and reveal the outcomes of their predictions.

The Element Explained

Foreshadowing occurs in literature when authors use clues or hints that suggest events that may happen later in the story. Recognizing these clues will help readers make reasonable predictions (a key reading strategy) while they read, as well as confirm or correct those same predictions. Understanding the literary element of foreshadowing requires that students become proficient at making predictions based on text clues.

Introducing the Literary Element

• Without showing students the book cover or title, read a portion of Karen Hesse's *Come On, Rain* (Scholastic, 1999) and ask students to identify clues in the text that lead them to believe an event is going to happen:

> *"I stare out over rooftops, past chimneys, into the way off distance. And that's when I see it coming, clouds rolling in, gray clouds, bunched and bulging under a purple sky."*

> Students should be able to explain that the words in the text foreshadow a storm.

• Show an age-appropriate movie or video clip. At certain intervals, stop the viewing and ask students to identify clues that indicate what events will happen next.

Modeling Activity

Tell or read a folktale in which an antagonist gets not what she or he wants, but what she or he deserves. One story you might consider is Margaret Reed MacDonald's *The Old Woman Who Lived in a Vinegar Bottle* (August House, 1997). After reading the story aloud, ask students to identify the clues in the text that foreshadowed the event in which the unlikable character received what she deserved.

Introducing the PowerPoint Activity

Tell students they will create a short PowerPoint presentation to show what they know about foreshadowing, using the book they've chosen (or you've assigned). Hand out copies of "Things to Come" (page 41) and review the steps and production guide. Show students the model PowerPoint presentation "Foreshadowing" from the CD.

Alternative Presentation

Challenge students to create a PowerPoint based on an O. Henry story in which all of the clues add up yet lead to a surprising conclusion. This requires students to use hindsight as they look carefully at the text clues. A good source to use for this activity is *Graphic Classics: O. Henry* (Eureka Productions, 2005).

Things to Come

PowerPoint Purpose

Explain the literary element of foreshadowing and provide text examples from your book. During your presentation, explain how you used these clues to make predictions about events that occurred later in the story.

Number of Slides

6 to 8 slides (If you need more or fewer slides, discuss options with your teacher.)

Creating the PowerPoint Presentation

1. Scan your book's cover or your own related artwork and insert the image into your opening *Title and Content* slide. Type the title "Foreshadowing" in the boxed area at the top of the slide.

2. Select the *Content with Caption* layout for the next slide. Insert the book cover image or artwork on the right side of the slide. On the left side, type the book's title in the smaller top box. Type the author's name, publisher, and copyright date in the larger box below it. Center the text and space the words out to make the whole slide look attractive.

3. Select a blank slide and insert a text box. Write a concise definition of the literary element "foreshadowing."

4. Add another blank slide and type a passage from the book illustrating foreshadowing. Make sure to use quotation marks and page number(s).

5. Repeat Step 4 to give another passage from the book that illustrates foreshadowing.

6. Repeat your opening slide to finish up your presentation.

Follow this basic format to meet the requirements for this assignment.

SLIDE 1: Book cover or artwork

SLIDE 2: Cover or art, title, author publisher, copyright date

Foreshadowing happens in a story when the author gives the reader hints or clues about what might happen next. If the reader picks up on these clues, she or he can make a good guess about what might happen.

In a really good story, readers are kind of "left up in the air," but they know **SOMETHING** is going to happen!

SLIDE 3: Definition of foreshadowing

On page 34, the text says that Johnny carries a six-inch switchblade in his back pocket because he was jumped by the Socs and badly beaten. The author foreshadows Johnny's use of his blade at some future time when she writes:

"He [Johnny] would kill the next person who jumped him. Nobody was ever going to beat him like that again. Not over his dead body ..."

SLIDE 4: First example of foreshadowing from the text

At the end of Chapter 3 in S.E. Hinton's *The Outsiders*, the narrator, Ponyboy, thinks to himself:

*"Things gotta get better, I figure.
They couldn't get worse. I was wrong."*

When Ponyboy thinks things couldn't get worse, the author is foreshadowing the fight in which Johnny kills Bob, and Ponyboy and Johnny must run away.

SLIDE 5: Second example of foreshadowing from the text

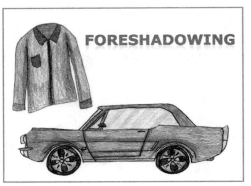

SLIDE 6: Final slide

Instant PowerPoint Lessons & Activities: Literary Elements © 2012 by Christine Boardman Moen, Scholastic Teaching Resources

Flashback

Going Back in Time

Students examine the use of flashback and provide examples from the text.

The Element Explained

Authors use *flashback* when they stop the action of a story to tell about an event that occurred at an earlier time. Used effectively, this literary device adds interest to the pacing of a story and adds depth to characters by giving readers needed information.

Introducing the Literary Element

• Invite students to read Aaron Elster's Holocaust survivor story, *I Still See Her Haunting Eyes* (BF Press, 2007), which is told using flashback. Alternatively, read aloud the picture book *Miss Rumphius* by Barbara Cooney (Puffin, 1985).

• Give students the poem template below. Encourage students to recall their past and use flashback as a writing technique to complete this free verse poem.

Now that I'm _____ , I like
    (insert age)

_____

_____ and

_____ .

But when I was half my age, I liked

_____

_____ and

_____ .

Modeling Activity

An effective way to teach flashback (and a good lesson in history) is to conduct an interview with a veteran and show the interview to students. Or, you might interview people in the community who can tell stories of how the community has changed. Stories of "I remember when . . ." will capture students' attention and provide examples of flashbacks.

Introducing the PowerPoint Activity

Tell students they will create a short PowerPoint presentation to show what they know about flashback, using the book they've chosen (or you've assigned). Hand out copies of "There and Back Again" (page 44) and review the steps and production guide. Show students the model PowerPoint presentation "Flashback" from the CD.

Alternative Presentation

If students are interested, you might have them create a PowerPoint presentation called "The Good Old Days," showing a flashback portrait of a time period, using informational texts.

There and Back Again

PowerPoint Purpose

Explain flashback and provide examples from your chosen text. During your presentation, explain how the author uses flashback to tell necessary story-related information and how the flashbacks relate to the main or ongoing story.

Number of Slides

10 to 15 slides (If you need more or fewer slides, discuss options with your teacher.)

Creating the PowerPoint Presentation

1. Scan your book's cover or your own related artwork and insert the image into your opening *Title and Content* slide. Type the title "Flashback" in the boxed area at the top of the slide.

2. Select the *Content with Caption* layout for the next slide. Insert the book cover image or artwork on the right side of the slide. On the left side, type the book's title in the smaller top box. Type the author's name, publisher, and copyright date in the larger box below it. Center the text and space the words out to make the whole slide look attractive.

3. Select a blank slide and insert a text box. Write a concise definition of the literary element "flashback."

4. Add another blank slide and insert a text box. Provide an example from the text that illustrates flashback. Insert a visual or picture using *Insert Picture*.

5. If necessary, use another blank slide to provide additional information or text support about your first example. Note the page number and/or chapter.

6. Repeat Steps 4 and 5 two more times to provide a second and a third example of flashback from the text.

7. On the next blank slide, summarize your flashback examples.

8. Repeat your opening slide to finish up your presentation.

Production Guide

Follow this basic format to meet the requirements for this assignment.

SLIDE 1: Book cover or artwork

SLIDE 2: Cover, title, author, publisher, copyright date

Instant PowerPoint Lessons & Activities: Literary Elements © 2012 by Christine Boardman Moen, Scholastic Teaching Resources

A **flashback** happens when the author stops telling the story to talk about events that happened earlier. A **flashback** may provide background information that helps the reader understand the story and its characters.

SLIDE 3: Definition of flashback

One flashback that occurs throughout the book is the story of Stanley's great-great-grandfather Eyla Yelnats and the curse that Madame Zeroni placed on him and his descendants.

This flashback is very important because without it, the story of Stanley and Zero would not make sense.

SLIDE 4: First example of flashback from text

Elya Yelnats, Stanley's relative, was cursed because he broke his promise to carry Madame Zeroni up the mountain and sing the song she had taught him. However, the curse is broken when Stanley carries Zero, whose real name is Hector Zeroni, up the mountain at Green Lake.

SLIDE 5: Additional information, if necessary

Another flashback happens in Chapter 23. The author tells about the history of Green Lake, which is a dried, dusty lake bed when Stanley first arrives at Green Lake Camp. This flashback is important because the reader is introduced to the characters of Miss Katherine Barlow, Trout Walker, and Onion Sam.

SLIDE 6: Second example of flashback from text

Another flashback occurs in Chapter 25. Readers learn about how Onion Sam and Miss Katherine fall in love, and she gives him peaches.

SLIDE 7: Third example of flashback from text

At that time period, their love was against the law. The townspeople burned the school. Sam was killed, and Miss Katherine became an outlaw called Kissin' Kate Barlow. This is also when Green Lake dried up for lack of rain.

SLIDE 8: Additional information, if necessary

The flashbacks help bring the story of Stanley Yelnats and Hector Zeroni full circle.

• Stanley breaks the family curse when he carries Hector up the mountain.

• Trout Walker is named as the man who killed Onion John and transformed Miss Katherine into an outlaw named Kissin' Kate Barlow.

• In the end the good guys win, and the bad guys lose. And rain finally comes to fill Green Lake once again.

SLIDE 9: Summary of flashbacks used in the text

Flashback

SLIDE 10: Final slide

Situational Irony

Expecting the Unexpected

Students explain situational irony, then provide examples from their book.

The Element Explained
Although verbal and dramatic irony are important literary elements, *situational irony* is often the type of irony students remember most because they enjoy a story that has an unexpected ending. In situational irony, the character(s) in the story as well as the reader usually do not expect the story's surprise outcome.

Introducing the Literary Element
• Younger students may enjoy the situational irony in David Small's classic book *Imogene's Antlers* (Macmillan, 1987) or Steven Kellogg's reissued version of *The Mysterious Tadpole* (Puffin, 2004). Both have unexpected twists at the end of their story. Older students may enjoy the short story "Charles" by Shirley Jackson, "The Interlopers" by Saki, or Allen Say's picture book *Grandfather's Journey* (Houghton Mifflin, 1993). After reading some of these stories aloud or having students read them to themselves or in groups, provide a definition of "situational irony" and explain how each story represents this literary element.

• When students have a grasp of situational irony, pose these questions: *Why would it be ironic if a postal worker forgot to put a stamp on a letter she or he mailed? Why would it be ironic for a dairy farmer to have a milk allergy?*

Modeling Activity
Put students in small groups or pairs and have them read O. Henry's short story "The Gift of the Magi." Have students complete the following statements:

Della sold her hair and bought Jim a chain for his watch. She expected to surprise him but _____. (Tell what happened instead.)

Jim sold his watch to buy combs for Della's hair. He expected to surprise her but _____. (Tell what happened instead.)

Thus the story's situational irony is _____.

Introducing the PowerPoint Activity
Tell students they will create a short PowerPoint presentation to show what they know about situational irony, using books and stories they've chosen (or you've assigned). Hand out copies of "Oh, the Irony!" (page 47) and review the steps and production guide. Show students the model PowerPoint presentation "Situational Irony" from the CD.

Alternative Presentation
Challenge students to take an existing story and insert situational irony to produce a surprise ending.

Oh, the Irony!

PowerPoint Purpose
Explain the literary element of situational irony and demonstrate how it is used in a short story, poem, or book you have read.

Number of Slides
8 to 10 slides (If you need more or fewer slides, discuss options with your teacher.)

Creating the PowerPoint Presentation

1. Scan your book's cover or your own related artwork and insert the image into the opening *Title and Content* slide. Type the title "Situational Irony" in the boxed area at the top of the slide.

2. Select the *Content with Caption* layout for the next slide. Insert the book cover image or artwork on the right side of the slide. On the left side, type the book's title in the smaller top box. Type the author's name, publisher, and copyright date in the larger box below it. Center the text and space the words out to make the whole slide look more attractive.

3. Select a blank slide and insert a text box. Write a concise definition of the literary element "situational irony."

4. Add another blank slide and insert a text box. Write a brief description of what the characters in the story expect to happen. In other words, explain the outcome the characters think will happen as a result of their actions.

5. Use another blank slide, if necessary, to explain more of your story and write a brief description of complications that arise during the story.

6. On the next blank slide, explain the situational irony or the unexpected outcome that surprises both the story's characters and the reader.

7. In simple terms, restate the situational irony that occurred in the story, book, or poem.

8. Repeat the opening slide to finish up your presentation.

Follow this basic format to meet the requirements for this assignment.

Situational Irony

SLIDE 1: Book cover or artwork

The Ransom of Red Chief

Author
O. Henry

Publisher
Eureka Productions

Copyright
2005

SLIDE 2: Cover, title, author, publisher, copyright date

Situational irony occurs when the events in a story lead to an unexpected or surprise ending. Both the reader and the character(s) are surprised by the unexpected outcome.

SLIDE 3: Definition of situational irony

In O. Henry's short story "The Ransom of Red Chief," two petty criminals cook up a scheme to kidnap the only son of the local banker in a sleepy town called Summit.

*   *   *   *   *   *   *

The criminals, Sam and Bill, think their plan is bound to work because they figure the banker has money to pay the ransom and he certainly would want his only son returned to him.

SLIDE 4: Explanation of character(s)' expected outcome

The ten-year-old boy Sam and Bill kidnap turns out to be quite a handful. Once they get the boy into camp, trouble begins. The boy:

• puts two buzzard feathers in his red hair and insists on being called Red Chief.

• jabbers nonstop and lets out loud WHOOPS.

• tries to scalp Bill and threatens to broil Sam at the stake.

• uses his sling-shot and hits Bill with a rock, knocking him out.

• wears out Bill with rough play and constant questions.

SLIDE 5: Description of plot complications

The situational irony occurs in the story when, instead of getting paid the $2,000 ransom, Bill and Sam end up paying Johnny's father $250 to take him back.

As Johnny's father explains in his "counterproposition," Bill and Sam should return Johnny at night because *"… the neighbors believe he is lost, and [he] couldn't be responsible for what they would do to anybody they saw bringing him back."*

(page 14)

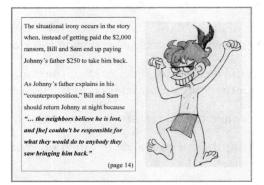

SLIDE 6: Explanation of situational irony from the text

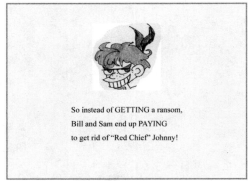

So instead of GETTING a ransom, Bill and Sam end up PAYING to get rid of "Red Chief" Johnny!

SLIDE 7: Restatement of the ironic situation

Situational Irony

SLIDE 8: Final slide

Symbolism

Stand-Ins

Students illustrate symbolism by explaining how the symbol is used in a story.

The Element Explained

Symbolism is a literary element in which something concrete, such as a person, place, or object, is used to represent something abstract—usually an idea, such as justice, or an emotion, such as determination. Real-life examples of symbols include a flag representing a country or the heart on a Valentine's Day card symbolizing love.

Introducing the Literary Element

Provide students with examples of symbols used in everyday life and also in literature. For example:

- Yellow flashing lights on a roadway symbolize "caution necessary." Ask students to list where yellow flashing lights are used in this fashion, such as on a school bus or in a construction zone.

- In parking lots, people recognize the spaces reserved for handicapped parking because of the symbol painted in the space or printed on the sign.

Invite students to draw common symbols and have other students identify their meaning.

Modeling Activity

Show students images of the Lady Justice from a book or the Internet. This symbolic figure is found in front of many court buildings. Explain the many symbols incorporated in this single figure—the double-edged sword in her right hand symbolizing reason and justice; the scale in her left hand representing the defense and prosecution, or opposite sides of a case; and the blindfold, which represents that justice should be "blind," meaning that justice should be fair and equal to all regardless of a person's power or position.

Introducing the PowerPoint Activity

Tell students that they will create a short PowerPoint presentation to show what they know about the use of symbols, using books, stories, or poems they've chosen (or you've assigned). Hand out copies of "Powerful Symbols" (page 50) and review the steps and production guide. Show students the model PowerPoint presentation "Symbolism" from the CD.

Alternative Presentation

Song lyrics often use symbolism. Using photographs, downloaded images, or created art, invite students to display song lyrics next to related, appropriate symbolic images.

Powerful Symbols

PowerPoint Purpose

Identify a symbol used in the literature that you have read and explain its meaning. Additionally, provide a concrete example of the symbol either through the use of a drawing, an illustration, a photograph, or a created object.

Number of Slides

7 to 10 slides (If you need more or fewer slides, discuss options with your teacher.)

Creating the PowerPoint Presentation

1. Scan your book's cover or your own related artwork and insert the image into the opening *Title and Content* slide. Type the title "Symbolism" in the boxed area at the top of the slide.

2. Select the *Content with Caption* layout for the next slide. Insert the book cover image or artwork on the right side of the slide. On the left side, type the book's title in the smaller top box. Type the author's name, publisher, and copyright date in the larger box below it. Center the text and space the words out to make the whole slide look attractive.

3. Select a blank slide and insert a text box. Write a concise definition of the literary element "symbolism."

4. Add another blank slide and insert a text box. Write an explanation of the significance of the symbol as it is used in the text. Use another blank slide if you need additional space for your explanation.

5. On the next blank slide, type a passage from the book that supports your explanation. Make sure to use quotation marks around the passage and to identify the page(s).

6. For the final slide, select the *Comparison* layout, which allows you to insert two images. Insert the book cover on one side and the image of the symbol on the other.

Instant PowerPoint Lessons & Activities: Literary Elements © 2012 by Christine Boardman Moen, Scholastic Teaching Resources

Follow this basic format to meet the requirements for this assignment.

SLIDE 1: Book cover or artwork

SLIDE 2: Cover, title, author, publisher, copyright date

Symbolism is the use of a person, object, or place to represent something else that is abstract, such as an idea or an emotion.

SLIDE 3: Definition of symbolism

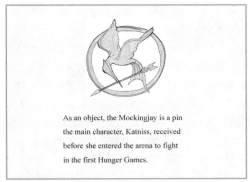

As an object, the Mockingjay is a pin the main character, Katniss, received before she entered the arena to fight in the first Hunger Games.

SLIDE 4: Explanation of symbol used in text

As a symbol, the Mockingjay represents the rebellion against the Capitol, which is the corrupt government. Eventually, Katniss dresses herself as the Mockingjay and represents the people's desire to rebel.

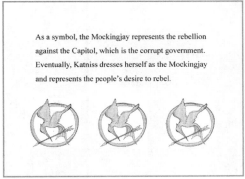

SLIDE 5: Further information about symbol in text

"The symbol of the revolution. The Mockingjay. It isn't enough, what I've done in the past, defying the Capitol in the Games, providing a rallying point. I must now become the actual leader, the face, the voice, the embodiment of the revolution."

(page 12)

SLIDE 6: Text support to explain symbol

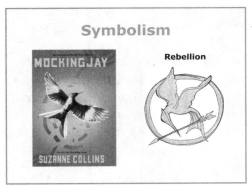

SLIDE 7: Text cover and symbol displayed side by side

Personification

Adding Life to a Story

Students examine how personification adds dimension to a story.

The Element Explained

Authors use *personification* when they give human qualities to animals, objects, or even ideas. By using personification, authors attempt to get the reader to view these animals, objects, or ideas in a different light, often with compassion or humor.

Introducing the Literary Element

- Remind students they are familiar with personification from animated movies they might have viewed. Have them give examples of such movies and name nonhuman characters that have been personified. Ask: *What human qualities do these "characters" exhibit?*

- Read aloud and show the illustrations from Maya Gottfried's book *Good Dog* (Dragonfly, 2008). Each dog's personality is portrayed through its brief monologue directed at its owner.

- Have students write "PERSONIFICATION" on a piece of paper and draw a box around the word *PERSON*. Next, invite students to make a list of human behaviors that indicate happiness, excitement, and fear. Divide the class into small groups and provide each group with illustrations, objects, photographs, or art books that depict inanimate objects, such as a pair of old shoes, an abandoned wagon, or a boat. Ask each group to select an object to "animate" using words from their lists. For example: *The weary, old shoes rested in the corner of the room after a long day of hard work in the fields.*

Modeling Activity

Make objects come to life using lively verbs in the following sentences.

> The old car engine _____ to life on the cold winter morning. (*sputtered, coughed*)
>
> The rusty hinge on the battered door _____ every time someone opened it. (*groaned, complained*)
>
> The curtains at the open window _____ with every breeze. (*danced, flounced*)

Introducing the PowerPoint Activity

Tell students they will create a short PowerPoint presentation to show what they know about personification, using the book they've chosen (or you've assigned). Hand out copies of "Personification Plus" (page 53) and review the steps and production guide. Show students the model PowerPoint presentation "Personification" from the CD.

Alternative Presentation

Have students write a brief poem or short story using personification. They can draw and scan in illustrations, add sound or voices, or create a video clip to insert into their PowerPoint presentation. Encourage students to use their imaginations to create presentations like "A Day in the Life of My Flip-Flops," "A Day in the Life of My Backpack," or "The Day the School Bus Spoke!"

Personification Plus

PowerPoint Purpose

Define personification and provide text examples to support your definition.

Number of Slides

8 to 10 slides (If you need more or fewer slides, discuss options with your teacher.)

Creating the PowerPoint

1. Scan your book's cover or your own related artwork and insert the image into your opening *Title and Content* slide. Type the title "Personification" in the boxed area at the top of the slide.

2. Select the *Content with Caption* layout for the next slide. Insert the book cover image or artwork on the right side of the slide. On the left side, type the book's title in the smaller top box. Type the author's name, publisher, and copyright date in the larger box below it. Center the text and space the words out to make the whole slide look attractive.

3. Select a blank slide and insert a text box. Write a concise definition of the literary element "personification."

4. Add another blank slide and use it to provide an easy reminder tip that the word *person* appears in the word *personification.*

5. On another blank slide, identify the object or idea that is being personified in your chosen text.

6. In the next blank slide, identify a passage from the text that illustrates personification. Make sure to use quotation marks and page number(s).

7. Repeat Step 6 to identify another passage from the text that illustrates personification.

8. Repeat the opening slide to finish up your presentation.

Instant PowerPoint Lessons & Activities: Literary Elements © 2012 by Christine Boardman Moen, Scholastic Teaching Resources

Follow this basic format to meet the requirements for this assignment.

SLIDE 1: Book cover or artwork

SLIDE 2: Cover, title, author, publisher, copyright date

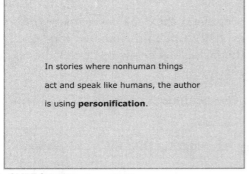

SLIDE 3: Definition of personification

In stories where nonhuman things act and speak like humans, the author is using **personification**.

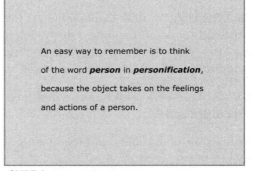

SLIDE 4: Memory tip: The word *person* in personification

An easy way to remember is to think of the word *person* in *personification*, because the object takes on the feelings and actions of a person.

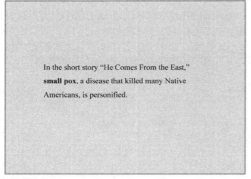

SLIDE 5: Explanation of what is being personified in the text

In the short story "He Comes From the East," **small pox**, a disease that killed many Native Americans, is personified.

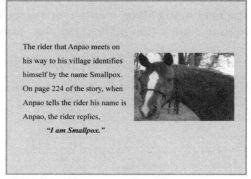

SLIDE 6: Example of personification from text

The rider that Anpao meets on his way to his village identifies himself by the name Smallpox. On page 224 of the story, when Anpao tells the rider his name is Anpao, the rider replies, *"I am Smallpox."*

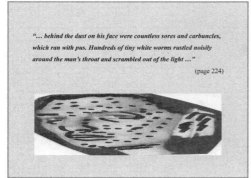

SLIDE 7: Second example of personification from text

"... behind the dust on his face were countless sores and carbuncles, which ran with pus. Hundreds of tiny white worms rustled noisily around the man's throat and scrambled out of the light ..." (page 224)

SLIDE 8: Final slide

Instant PowerPoint Lessons & Activities: Literary Elements © 2012 by Christine Boardman Moen, Scholastic Teaching Resources

Simile

Like a Metaphor, But Not

Students examine the use of similes and explain the comparisons being made.

The Element Explained

A *simile* compares two unlike things, often by using the words *like* and *as*. Authors use similes to create images in readers' minds. An example of a famous simile is the title and first line of Robert Burns's famous poem "My Love Is Like a Red, Red Rose." Students, however, might appreciate a sports-related simile such as, "She was so ecstatic about winning the race, her heart pounded like the band's bass drum."

Introducing the Literary Element

• Invite students to identify the two objects being compared in the following similes. Use the frame provided so that students recognize that similes use the words *like* and *as*.

Lava flowed down the sides of the volcano like ice cream down a cone.

_____ like _____

The cryptic message was as puzzling as a knotted-up necklace.

_____ as _____

The tall paper cups at the coffee shop looked like soldiers standing at attention.

_____ like _____

• Rewriting clichés that sometimes find their way into students' writing is a good way to teach students to recognize and revise overworked expressions. Present the following list and ask students to rewrite each cliché using a better simile.

Without his glasses, he was as blind as a bat.

The shy boy was as quiet as a mouse.

The embarrassed student looked like a deer caught in the headlights.

Modeling Activity

In Kalli Dakos's poem "Imaginary Friends," from her book *The Goof Who Invented Homework* (Dial, 1996), the author uses the simile, "I felt like a crayon in a box of pencils." Everyone feels odd or left out or like a misfit at one time or another. Invite students to write original similes by completing the stem, "I felt like . . ." For example: *I felt like a tadpole in a tank full of sharks. I felt like a frame without any picture. I felt like a basketball in the middle of a golf course.*

Introducing the PowerPoint Activity

Tell students they will create a short PowerPoint presentation to show what they know about similes, using books and poems they've chosen (or you've assigned). Hand out copies of "As Simple as a Simile" (page 56) and review the steps and production guide. Show students the model PowerPoint presentation "Simile" from the CD.

Alternative Presentation

Have students collect similes from many sources and weave them together into an original poem or song lyrics. This would be similar to creating a Dada poem.

As Simple as a Simile

PowerPoint Purpose
Provide at least three examples from a text or texts illustrating an author's use of simile. Explain the two objects being compared in each simile.

Number of Slides
6 to 9 slides (If you need more or fewer slides, discuss options with your teacher.)

Creating the PowerPoint Presentation

1. Insert a scanned image of an eye-catching artwork you've created into your opening *Title and Content* slide. Type the title "Simile" in the boxed area at the top of the slide. (The artwork used on the sample PowerPoint was created using wordle.net's "word clouds," but you can create the same "word art" using other programs.)

2. Select a blank slide and insert a text box. Write a concise definition of "simile." If you wish, you may include an additional slide to emphasize an author's purpose in using simile in his or her writing.

3. In the next blank slide, provide an example of a simile from a text. Explain the two objects being compared. Using the *Insert Picture* command, put the cover image of the text from which you found the simile or a related photo or artwork.

4. Repeat Step 3 two times to give two more examples of a simile from either the same text or a different one. Make sure to explain the two objects being compared in both examples.

5. Repeat your opening slide to finish up your presentation.

Instant PowerPoint Lessons & Activities: Literary Elements © 2012 by Christine Boardman Moen, Scholastic Teaching Resources

Follow this basic format to meet the requirements for this assignment.

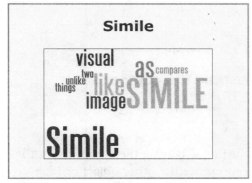

SLIDE 1: Created art to introduce simile

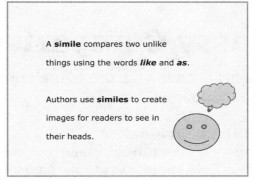

SLIDE 2: Definition of simile (Use an additional slide if you wish to explain author's purpose.)

SLIDE 3: First example of simile, explanation, image

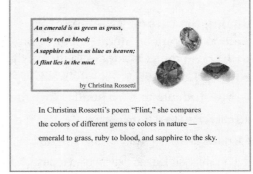

SLIDE 4: Second example of simile, explanation, image

SLIDE 5: Third example of simile, explanation, image

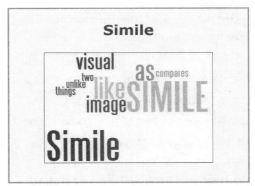

SLIDE 6: Final slide

Metaphor

Classy Comparisons

Students examine the use of metaphor and illustrate the comparison being made.

The Element Explained

A *metaphor* is a comparison between two unlike objects or ideas. During the comparison, the objects or ideas "switch places," and one object or idea represents the other object or idea. A simile, also a comparison, uses the words *like* or *as*. Metaphors do not use these terms in their comparisons.

Introducing the Literary Element

• Read aloud "Metaphor" and "Pinball" from Ralph Fletcher's *A Writing Kind of Day* (Boyds Mill Press, 2005) and ask students to identify the use of metaphor. For older students, read "Hope Is the Thing With Feathers" by Emily Dickinson or "Mother to Son" by Langston Hughes.

• Challenge students to turn similes into metaphors. Start with this list:

> Her smile was like a frozen pond.
>
> He fidgeted like a dog with fleas.
>
> Her long wet hair looked like tangled ropes.

Modeling Activity

Invite students to describe themselves using metaphors that begin with the stem: *I am* _____.
One student's example was:

> I am wind.
>
> I rush down the basketball court.
>
> I float to the basket.
>
> I hear the swish of the ball as it goes through the hoop.
>
> I am wind.

Introducing the PowerPoint Activity

Tell students they will create a short PowerPoint presentation to show what they know about metaphors, using the book or text they've chosen (or you've assigned). Hand out copies of "Metaphorically Speaking" (page 59) and review the steps and production guide. Show students the model PowerPoint presentation "Metaphor" from the CD.

Alternative Presentation

Have students write metaphors that characterize some aspect of a book they have read. For example, after reading *Night* (Hill and Wang, 2006), a classic Holocaust survival memoir by Elie Wiesel, a student wrote, "Hope is a battered cup and a bent spoon" to describe a scene in the book.

Metaphorically Speaking

PowerPoint Purpose
Define metaphor, provide examples of metaphor from a text or texts, and explain what is being compared in the metaphor(s).

Number of Slides
8 to 10 slides (If you need more or fewer slides, discuss options with your teacher.)

Creating the PowerPoint

1. Scan your book's cover or your own related artwork and insert the image into your opening *Title and Content* slide. Type the title "Metaphor" in the boxed area at the top of the slide.

2. Select the *Content with Caption* layout for the next slide. Insert the book cover image or artwork on the right side of the slide. On the left side, type the book's title in the smaller top box. Type the author's name, publisher, and copyright date in the larger box below it. Center the text and space the words out to make the whole slide look attractive.

3. Select a blank slide and insert a text box. Write a definition of "metaphor" and provide a brief example.

4. Add another blank slide and insert a text box. Provide the first example of metaphor. Explain the two unlike objects being compared. If you wish to insert art or visuals on your slide, use the *Insert Picture* option.

5. Repeat Step 4 two more times to provide a second and third example of metaphor.

6. Repeat your opening slide to finish up your presentation.

Follow this basic format to meet the requirements for this assignment.

SLIDE 1: Book cover or artwork

SLIDE 2: Cover, title, author, publisher, copyright date

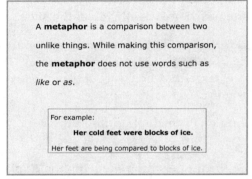

SLIDE 3: Definition of metaphor

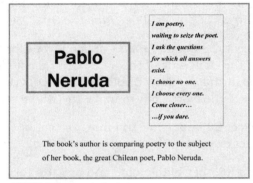

SLIDE 4: First example of metaphor

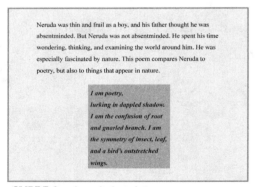

SLIDE 5: Second example of metaphor

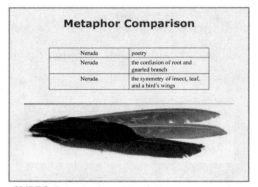

SLIDE 6: Explanation of second example, if necessary

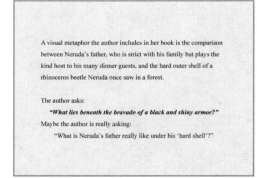

SLIDE 7: Third example of metaphor

SLIDE 8: Final slide

Instant PowerPoint Lessons & Activities: Literary Elements © 2012 by Christine Boardman Moen, Scholastic Teaching Resources

Alliteration

Excellent Examples

Students share examples of alliteration from their favorite poems.

The Element Explained
Alliteration is the repetition of the same sound in words that are placed closely together. The sound usually repeated is the initial sounds like those found in tongue-twisters. Artfully employed, alliteration can impact a story or poem's mood.

Introducing the Literary Element
• Following the pattern in Laura Vaccaro Seeger's book *Walter Was Worried* (Roaring Brook Press, 2005), have students write their own alliteration statements using their names. For example, *"Walter was worried when . . ." "Priscilla was puzzled when . . ."* Students may even wish to pattern their illustrated name-alliteration statements by using the letters of the alliterations to form facial expressions just as Seeger did in her book.

• Invite students to write an alliteration statement on a note card using the name of the main character in their independent reading book. Instruct students to slip the note card in front of their books and then have a "book pass" in which the books get passed around the room to classmates. Students pull out the alliteration statements and read about the main character. For example, for Jerry Spinelli's book *Crash* (Knopf, 1996), a student might write: "Crash Coogan could crush a can completely."

Modeling Activity
Write the letters of the alphabet on slips of paper and put them in a paper bag. Have students draw a letter from the bag and write an alliterative tongue-twister using that letter. Once completed, you might compile the tongue-twisters into a simple book or post them on a bulletin board. One student example is: "Wacky Willis waxed wheezing whales, wondering whether or not Willy Wonka's wafers were wonderful."

Introducing the PowerPoint Activity
Tell students they will create a short PowerPoint presentation to show what they know about alliteration, using books and poems they've chosen (or you've assigned). Hand out copies of "Alliteration Alert!" (page 62) and review the steps and production guide. Show students the model PowerPoint presentation "Alliteration" from the CD.

Alternative Presentation
Challenge students to change portions of texts, including lines from poems, to include alliteration. In the presentation, have students first show the original text, and then display the revised text that includes examples of alliteration.

Alliteration Alert!

PowerPoint Purpose
Define alliteration and provide examples from poetry books.

Number of Slides
9 to 15 slides (If you need more or fewer slides, discuss options with your teacher.)

Creating the PowerPoint Presentation

1. Select the *Title Only* layout for your opening slide. Type the title "Alliteration" in the top box. Then insert a text box below to create an opening banner, headline, or statement about alliteration.

2. Select a blank slide and insert a text box. Write a concise definition of "alliteration."

3. On another blank slide, provide an example of a tongue-twister.

4. Select the *Content with Caption* layout for the next slide. Scan the cover of a poetry book that contains an example of alliteration or your own related artwork. Insert the image on the right side of the slide. On the left side, type the book's title in the smaller top box. Type the author's name, publisher, and copyright date in the larger box below it. Center the text and space the words out to make the whole slide look attractive.

5. On the next blank slide, provide an example of alliteration from one of the poems in the collection of poems you have chosen.

6. Repeat Steps 4 and 5 to show another poem and another example of alliteration. If this second poem comes from a different book, scan and insert the book's cover.

7. Add another blank slide and introduce a humorous poem from which you will select an example of alliteration.

8. If you want, provide the humorous alliteration example on another blank side.

9. Repeat your opening slide to finish up your presentation.

Production Guide
Follow this basic format to meet the requirements for this assignment.

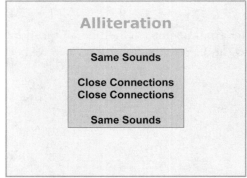

Alliteration

Same Sounds

Close Connections
Close Connections

Same Sounds

SLIDE 1: Opening slide with banner and the word *alliteration*

Authors use **alliteration** when they use words that repeat the same sounds. "Same sounds" is an example of **alliteration**. Usually the words with the same sound are close together, but they don't have to be.

SLIDE 2: Definition of alliteration

Instant PowerPoint Lessons & Activities: Literary Elements © 2012 by Christine Boardman Moen, Scholastic Teaching Resources

Familiar tongue-twisters are also examples of alliteration.

Sally sold sea shells by the seashore.

The "S" is repeated to create the alliteration.

SLIDE 3: Tongue-twister example of alliteration

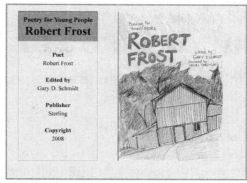

SLIDE 4: Cover, title, author, publisher, copyright date

Going for Water
by Robert Frost

We ran as if to meet the moon
That slowly danced behind the trees,
The barren boughs without the leaves,
Without the birds, without the breeze.

SLIDE 5: Example of alliteration from text

SLIDE 6: Cover, title, author, publisher, copyright date

A soft sea washed around the house,
A sea of summer air
And rose and fell the magic planks
That sailed without a care.

By Emily Dickinson

SLIDE 7: Example of alliteration from text

Humorous poets such as Jack Prelutsky and Shel Silverstein often used alliteration in their poems.

Jack Prelutsky's poem "The Giggling Gaggling Gaggle of Geese" is a good example.

SLIDE 8: Other poets and/or poems that have humorous alliteration

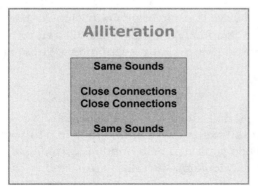

SLIDE 9: Final slide

Instant PowerPoint Lessons & Activities: Literary Elements © 2012 by Christine Boardman Moen, Scholastic Teaching Resources

Puns and Onomatopoeia

Sounds Like Fun!

Students provide examples of homophonic and homographic puns as well as onomatopoeia.

The Element Explained

A *pun* is a play on words. Authors use puns for humor. *Homographic puns* use the same word that has two different meanings. For example: *How do you know you can always rely on a horse? It's a stable animal. Homophonic puns* are based on words that sound similar but have different meanings. For example: *When it rains like cats and dogs outside, be careful not to step into any poodles. Onomatopoeia* refers to a word that imitates or suggests different sounds. Words such as *crash*, *boom*, and *buzz* suggest the action and sound of the things themselves.

Introducing the Literary Element

• Read several puns from various joke books. Ask students to explain how the dual use of the word(s) creates the humor. Identify each as a homographic or homophonic pun.

• Distribute to students different editions of newspaper comic pages, age-appropriate graphic novels, or comic-strip collection books, such as *Peanuts* or *Calvin and Hobbes*. Ask students to find the "sound words" inserted into the stories or comic strips. Compile a list of onomatopoeic words from the texts and invite students to add their own to the list.

Modeling the Activity

• Arrange students in groups of three. Provide each group with books of jokes, riddles, puns, and a sticky note. Have each group select one pun and tag it with their names. Invite the groups to take turns reading their puns. One member reads aloud the pun, joke, or riddle, another identifies and explains the word(s) being used to create the pun, and the third explains how the word(s) is used as a pun—either homographic or homophonic.

• Keeping students in the same groups, have them create a story brief enough to be told in three minutes or less and that includes three different sound effects. Before they begin, discuss possible characters, settings, conflicts, and plot lines. Refer to the list of suitable onomatopoeias you generated earlier (see "Introducing the Literary Element"). Allow groups time to create, rehearse, and perform their stories.

Introducing the PowerPoint Activity

Tell students they will create a short PowerPoint presentation to show what they know about onomatopoeia and puns from books or graphic novels they've chosen (or you've assigned). Hand out copies of "Fun Puns" (page 65) and "Onomatopoeia? Sounds Like Fun!" (page 68) and review the steps and production guides. Show students the model PowerPoint presentations "Puns" and "Onomatopoeia" from the CD.

Alternative Presentation

Have students write and illustrate their own comic strips that include onomatopoeia and write and illustrate their own puns. Another alternative is to have students rewrite puns they find in books and illustrate them to explain the puns' meanings. A good source to help budding cartoonists is *KA-BOOM! A Dictionary of Comic Book Words, Symbols & Onomatopoeia* (Mora Publications, 2007).

Fun Puns

PowerPoint Purpose
Provide examples and explanations of homographic and homophonic puns from poems, jokes, graphic novels, and other text types.

Number of Slides
13 to 15 slides (If you need more or fewer slides, discuss options with your teacher.)

Creating the PowerPoint Presentation

1. Select the *Title Only* layout for your opening slide. Type the title "Pun" in the top box. Then insert a text box below to create an opening banner, headline, or statement about puns.

2. Select a blank slide and insert a text box. Write a concise definition of "pun" and identify the two types of puns.

3. Add another blank slide and provide the definition of a homographic pun.

4. Select the *Content with Caption* layout for the next slide. Scan the cover of a book that contains an example of a homographic pun or scan your own related artwork. Insert the image on the right side of the slide. On the left side, type the book's title in the smaller top box. Type the author's name, publisher, and copyright date in the larger box below it. Center the text and space the words out to make the whole slide look attractive.

5. Add a blank slide and provide an example of a homographic pun from the book.

6. Use another blank slide if you need to explain the pun further or to illustrate the pun.

7. On another blank slide, insert a text box and provide the definition of a homophonic pun.

8. Repeat Steps 4 to 6 for a book that contains an example of a homophonic pun.

9. Repeat your opening slide to finish up your presentation.

Follow this basic format to meet the requirements for this assignment.

SLIDE 1: Opening slide using a banner: Puns Are Fun!

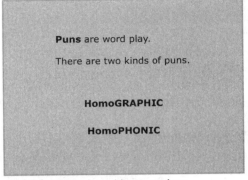

SLIDE 2: Definition of pun and the two types of puns

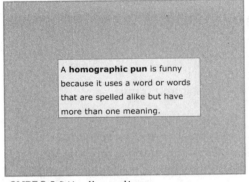

SLIDE 3: Definition of homographic pun

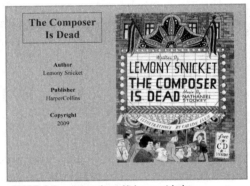

SLIDE 4: Cover, title, author, publisher, copyright date

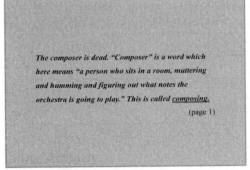

SLIDE 5: Example of homographic pun from text

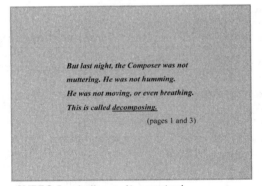

SLIDE 6: Example of homographic pun continued

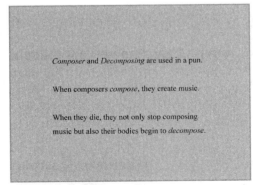

SLIDE 7: Explanation of homographic pun

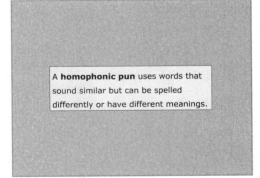

SLIDE 8: Definition of homophonic pun

Instant PowerPoint Lessons & Activities: Literary Elements © 2012 by Christine Boardman Moen, Scholastic Teaching Resources

SLIDE 9: Cover, title, author, publisher, copyright date

SLIDE 10: Example of homophonic pun from text

SLIDE 11: Example of homophonic pun continued

SLIDE 12: Explanation of homophonic pun and/or illustration

SLIDE 13: Final slide

Onomatopoeia? Sounds Like Fun!

PowerPoint Purpose

Provide examples and explanations of onomatopoeia from poems, jokes, graphic novels, or other text types.

Number of Slides

8 to 10 slides (If you need more or fewer slides, discuss options with your teacher.)

Creating the PowerPoint Presentation

1. Select the *Title Only* layout for your opening slide. Type the title "Onomatopoeia" in the top box. Then insert a text box below to create an opening banner, headline, or statement about onomatopoeia.

2. Select a blank slide and insert a text box. Write a concise definition of "onomatopoeia."

3. Add another blank slide and list examples of onomatopoeia.

4. Select the *Content with Caption* layout for the next slide. Scan your book's cover or your own related artwork and insert the image on the right side of the slide. On the left side, type the book's title in the smaller top box. Type the author's name, publisher, and copyright date in the larger box below it. Center the text and space the words out to make the whole slide look attractive.

5. On the next blank slide, provide examples of onomatopoeia from the book.

6. Add another blank slide and use the *Insert Picture* command to add the cover of a graphic novel that contains onomatopoeia. Insert a text box next to the cover and identify the author, publisher, and copyright date of the book. Explain that graphic novels often use onomatopoeia.

7. On another blank slide, insert a scanned image of a page from a graphic novel that includes onomatopoeia. List the examples of onomatopoeia on the right side of the slide using a text box.

8. Repeat your opening slide to finish up your presentation.

Follow this basic format to meet the requirements for this assignment.

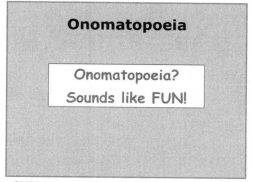

SLIDE 1: Opening slide using a banner

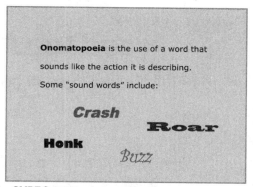

SLIDE 2: Definition of onomatopoeia

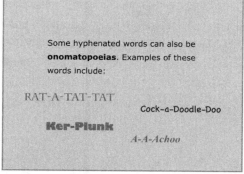

SLIDE 3: Examples of onomatopoeia

SLIDE 4: Cover, title, author, publisher, copyright date

SLIDE 5: Examples listed from text

SLIDE 6: Graphic novel cover, author, publisher, copyright date

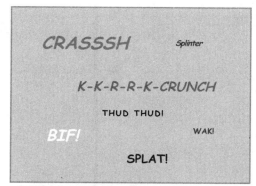

SLIDE 7: Examples listed from graphic novel

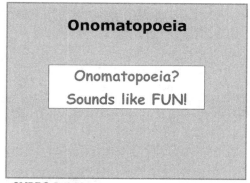

SLIDE 8: Final slide

Appendix

Command Central

Use these keystrokes and screens to help create your PowerPoint presentations.

Slides

You can use three basic slide layouts when creating your PowerPoint presentation. Other layouts are available if you wish to use them, but these slides are all that you need.

Title and Content

Title and Content Use this layout as your opening slide, in which you can insert the name of the literary element, as well as the book cover or cover art.

Content with Caption

Content with Caption This "split screen" layout allows you to insert the book cover or cover art side-by-side with the author's name, the book's publisher, and copyright date.

Blank

Blank With this versatile layout, you can insert a text box and/or an image or picture, if you wish (using the *Insert Picture* command).

Instant PowerPoint Lessons & Activities: Literary Elements © 2012 by Christine Boardman Moen, Scholastic Teaching Resources

Keystroke Commands

There are eight basic keystroke commands that you will use to create your presentation. The "ribbon" or tool bar that runs across the top of the screen while you are creating your PowerPoint looks like this:

FILE   Home   Insert   Design   Transitions   Animations   Slide Show   Review   View

Insert a new slide	New Slide ▾	On the Home tab, click *Insert New Slide*. Select *Layout* to choose the slide design you wish to use.
Insert a picture	Picture	Click on the Insert tab, then click on the *Picture* icon on the left to open the list of scanned images you have saved. Select the title of the image you wish to insert into your PowerPoint presentation, then click *Insert* to import the image.
Resize or move an image		To resize an image, put the cursor on the outline box of the image until the cursor turns into a two-headed arrow. You can make the image larger or smaller by dragging this arrow. To move an image, place the cursor on the image until it turns into a four-headed arrow. Using this arrow, you can drag any object or image to a new location on your slide.
Insert a text box	A Text Box	To insert a text box, click on the *Insert* tab and select *Text Box*. As you type your text into the box, the box will grow. You can change font size and line spacing by clicking on the words *Font* and *Paragraph* that appear at the bottom of the ribbon or tool bar. To move the text box anywhere on the slide, hold down the cursor on the text box border until it becomes a four-headed arrow, then drag the box around.
Delete text and images		To delete text within a text box, click on the text then on the border of the text box. Then press the delete button. To delete an image, click on the image and hit the delete button.
Check spelling	ABC Spelling	Check for correct spelling throughout your presentation by clicking on the *Review* tab. The word *Spelling* will appear on the far left. Click on this word to review the text in your slide show.
Save your PowerPoint	Save / Save As	Use the *File* tab and scroll down to *Save As*. When you click on *Save As*, a screen will appear. Give your presentation a name, such as MOOD, and save it as a PowerPoint presentation.
Full-screen mode	From Beginning	To show your PowerPoint during your oral presentation, click on *Slide Show*. The words *From Beginning* will appear on the left. Click on these words, and your slide show will appear in full-screen mode. To advance to the next slide, right click on the mouse and the next slide will appear.

Technology Tips

If you would like to take advantage of PowerPoint's other features, the technology tips below can help. However, before you add every bell and whistle to your slide show, make sure to first evaluate each feature to determine its usefulness given the objective of your project. Some features, such as cascading letters and multicolored slides, may be fun, but unless they have a specific purpose, these extra features may actually detract from your presentation and make it less appealing. Have fun and be creative, but don't lose track of the primary purpose of your PowerPoint project.

Adding Color to Selected Slides
- On the tool bar or ribbon, select the *Design* option.
- To the far right, select *Background Styles*. Colored slides will appear.
- Click on the color you wish to select, then left-click your mouse.
- Select *Apply to Selected Slides*.

Inserting an Audio Clip
- Select a slide with a media icon from *Home* on the tool bar or ribbon.
- Select the *Insert* option on the tool bar or ribbon.
- Select the *Audio* icon from the tool bar or ribbon then scroll down and select *Audio from File*.
- A small window will appear on the left of your screen. Select *Music* from the list of available options.
- The song titles in your music library will appear. Select a song and click *Insert*. (You must record or "rip" songs onto your computer first in order to use this feature.)
- The *Audio* icon will appear on your slide. To play the song, click on the left arrow below the icon. You can move the icon to any place on the screen. During your slide show, click on the icon to play the music clip.

Inserting a Video Clip
- Use a Flip™ camcorder or other digital video-recording device to record your video.
- Save your video clips to your computer.
- Select a slide that has a media clip icon. When you select the media icon on the slide, the *Insert Video* box appears. Go to your list of videos, select one, and click *Insert*. The video clip will be added to your presentation.
- The video in your presentation should play when you double-click on the slide.

Instant PowerPoint Lessons & Activities: Literary Elements © 2012 by Christine Boardman Moen, Scholastic Teaching Resources

General Guidelines for Fair Use of Copyrighted Materials

Category	Acceptable	Unacceptable	Creative Solutions
Text including • poems • newspaper articles • books • magazines • any other text whether in paper format or digital format	• You may use an entire poem in your PowerPoint presentation if the poem consists of fewer than 250 words. • If the poem has more than 2500 words, you may use 250 words from the poem in your presentation. • You may use portions of a text to support your analysis in your presentation. You may use up to 10 percent or a thousand words.	You may not reproduce an entire text for any reason. Since PowerPoint presentations should not be "text heavy," this should not be a difficult guideline to follow.	Often you will need to use direct quotations from your book or other text to support the analysis of your literary element. However, writing a summary or paraphrasing using your own words can be just as effective when describing a scene, a character, or a plot event.
Images including • photographs • illustrations • pictures • charts • diagrams • graphs • cartoons • Web pages	• One per book, encyclopedia, newspaper, or magazine of any chart, picture, graph, diagram, or cartoon. • No more than five photographs or illustrations by the same photographer or illustrator.	• You may not use copyrighted logos of products without permission. • You may not scan pictures or illustrations from an entire picture book and use them in your PowerPoint presentation.	• Shoot your own photographs and use those instead of the ones in the text. • Draw your own charts, diagrams, graphs, and cartoons. • Dress up your presentation by drawing your own illustrations to accompany the text.

General Guidelines for Fair Use of Copyrighted Materials (continued)

Category	Acceptable	Unacceptable	Creative Solutions
Music	• You may use 10 percent of any copyrighted song or other works of music such as musicals, symphonies, or concerts. • An often-used guideline is to use no more than 30 seconds of any one musical work.	• You may not insert an entire song to play as background music for your PowerPoint presentation. • You may not "chop up" an entire song into 30-second portions and insert those sound pieces into your PowerPoint presentation.	• Create your own original sound effects to use in your presentation. • Write your own songs or musical accompaniment.
Video including • **television shows** • **news programs** • **commercials** • **DVDs** • **Internet video that is copyrighted**	You may use up to 10 percent, but no more than 3 minutes (whichever is less), of any television show, DVD, or Internet clip.	You may not show an entire cartoon, commercial, or video short.	Use a digital movie camera and create your own video clips to insert into your PowerPoint presentation.

Instant PowerPoint Lessons & Activities: Literary Elements © 2012 by Christine Boardman Moen, Scholastic Teaching Resources

Resources

Character
The Hunger Games trilogy by Suzanne Collins (Scholastic, 2010)

Sassy: Little Sister Is NOT My Name by Sharon M. Draper (Scholastic, 2009)

Setting
The Watsons Go to Birmingham—1963 by Christopher Paul Curtis (Yearling, 1997)

Plot
The Houdini Box by Brian Selznick (Atheneum, 1991)

Theme
Aesop's Fables

       "The Fox and the Stork"

       "The Lion and the Mouse"

       "The Boy who Cried Wolf"

Armadilly Chili by Helen Ketterman (Whitman, 2004)

Middle School Is Worse Than Meatloaf by Jennifer L. Holm (Atheneum, 2007)

Sélavi, That is Life: A Haitian Story of Hope by Youme Landowne (Cinco Puntos Press, 2005)

Swear to Howdy by Wendelin Van Draanen (Yearling, 2005)

Conflict
Art & Max by David Wiesner (Clarion, 2010)

The Buffalo Are Back by Jean Craighead George (Dutton, 2010)

Dave the Potter: Artist, Poet, Slave by Laban Carrick Hill (Little, Brown, 2010)

Elsie's Bird by Jane Yolen (Philomel, 2010)

Trouble by Gary D. Schmidt (Clarion, 2008)

Point of View
14 Cows for America by Carmen Agra Deedy (Peachtree, 2009)

The Danger Box by Blue Balliett (Scholastic, 2010)

Gossamer by Lois Lowry (Yearling, 2008)

Henry's Freedom Box by Ellen Levine (Scholastic, 2007)

How to Survive in Antarctica by Lucy Jane Bledsoe (Holiday House, 2006)

Yatandou by Gloria Whelan (Sleeping Bear Press, 2007)

You by Charles Benoit (HarperTeen, 2010)

Mood
Deep and Dark and Dangerous by Mary Downing Hahn (Clarion, 2007)

Foreshadowing
Come On, Rain! by Karen Hesse (Scholastic, 1999)

The Old Woman Who Lived in a Vinegar Bottle by Margaret Read MacDonald (August House, 2005)

The Outsiders by S. E. Hinton (Viking Press, 1967)

Flashback
Holes by Louis Sachar (Yearling, 2000)

I Still See Her Haunting Eyes by Aaron Elster (BF Press, 2007)

Miss Rumphius by Barbara Cooney (Puffin, 1985)

Situational Irony
"Charles," short story by Shirley Jackson

"The Interlopers," short story by Saki

Grandfather's Journey by Allen Say (Houghton Mifflin, 1993)

Graphic Classics: O. Henry (Eureka Productions, 2005)
> "The Gift of the Magi"
> "The Ransom of Red Chief"

Imogene's Antlers by David Small (Dragonfly, 1988)

The Mysterious Tadpole by Steven Kellogg (Puffin, 2004)

Symbolism
Mockingjay by Suzanne Collins (Scholastic, 2010)

Personification
Anpao by Jamake Highwater (HarperCollins, 1992)

Good Dog by Maya Gottfried (Dragonfly, 2008)

Simile
The Goof Who Invented Homework: and Other School Poems by Kalli Dakos (Dial, 1996)

Heart to Heart: New Poems Inspired by Twentieth-Century American Art by Jan Greenberg (Abrams, 2001)

Poems From Homeroom: A Writer's Place to Start by Kathi Appelt (Henry Holt, 2002)

Steady Hands: Poems About Work by Tracie Vaughn Zimmer (Clarion, 2009)

Metaphor

A Writing Kind of Day: Poems for Young Poets by Ralph Fletcher (Boyds Mills Press, 2005)

The Dreamer by Pam Muñoz Ryan (Scholastic, 2010)

Night by Elie Wiesel (Hill and Wang, 2006)

Poetry for Young People: Emily Dickinson edited by Frances Schoonmaker Bolin (Sterling, 2008)

Poetry for Young People: Langston Hughes edited by David Roessel and Arnold Rampersad (Sterling, 2006)

Alliteration

"The Giggling Gaggling Gaggle of Geese," poem by Jack Prelutsky

Crash by Jerry Spinelli (Knopf, 1996)

Poetry for Young People: Robert Frost edited by Gary D. Schmidt (Sterling, 2008)

Walter Was Worried by Laura Vaccaro Seeger (Roaring Brook Press, 2006)

Puns and Onomatopoeia

Bone by Jeff Smith (Scholastic, 2005)

The Complete Calvin and Hobbes by Bill Watterson (McMeel, 2005)

The Composer Is Dead by Lemony Snicket (HarperCollins, 2009)

KA-BOOM! A Dictionary of Comic Book Words, Symbols & Onomatopoeia by Kevin Taylor (Lulu.com, 2007)

Peanuts 2000 by Charles M. Schulz (Ballantine, 2000)

Puns and Games by Richard Lederer (Chicago Review Press, 1996)

R Is for Rhyme: A Poetry Alphabet by Judy Young (Sleeping Bear Press, 2010)

Notes